Imam Nawawī's collection of
FORTY ḤADĪTH

Imam Nawawī's collection of

FORTY
ḤADĪTH

Arabic Text, Translation and Notes

Islamic Book Trust, Kuala Lumpur

© Islamic Book Trust, Kuala Lumpur 1996
ISBN 983-9154-03-6

First reprint 2001

Published by
Islamic Book Trust
607 Mutiara Majestic
Jalan Othman
46000 Petaling Jaya
Selangor, Malaysia.

Email: ibtkl@pd.jaring.my
Website: www.ibtbooks.com

Printed by
Academy Art & Printing Services Sdn. Bhd.
Kuala Lumpur

Contents

Imam Nawawī

A short biography

Imam Muhyī al-Dīn Abū Zakarīya Yahyā bin Sharaf al-Nawawī, for short Imam Nawawī, was born in the village of Nawa in the vicinity of Damascus in 631 A.H. (1233 A.D.). He grew up in Nawa and at the age of nineteen moved into Damascus where he completed his studies and later wrote and taught on all the subjects which were then current among religious scholars of that age. At one time he was attracted to the study of medicine but soon abandoned the attempt as he thought that it would distract his mind and wean it away from the study and pursuit of subjects in which he was more vitally interested. Imam Nawawī led a life of singular piety, righteousness, simplicity and concentration on the spiritual. He left behind a large number of valuable works on different topics, among them are *Riyād al-Sālihīn, Sharh Sahīh Muslim, al-Adhkar, al-Tibyān fī adāb hamalat al-Qur'ān, al-Irshād wa'l-Taqrīb fī 'Ulūm al-Hadīth, al-Minhāj* and many others. His *Sharh Muslim* is a standard text book for the study of Hadīth while his *al-Minhāj* on study of *Fiqh*. This collection of Forty Hadīth is the translation of his *Matan al-Arba'īn.*

Imam Nawawī, the saintly scholar, died at the early age of forty-six in 676 A.H. (1278 A.D.) in the village of his birth, and was deeply mourned by all sections of Muslim society in Damascus.

Introduction[*]

In the name of Allah,
Most Gracious, Most Merciful

Praise be to Allah, Lord of the worlds, eternal Guardian of the heavens and the earths, Ruler over all creatures, who sent to responsible beings the Messengers—upon whom be His blessing and peace—that they might bring them guidance and make clear to them the *Sharī'ah* (Law). Him do I praise for all His favours, and from Him do I beg increase of His kindness and His generosity. Also I bear witness that our Master Muhammad is His servant and His Messenger, His Beloved and His friend, the most excellent of created beings, who was honoured by being given the mighty Qur'an, and by being given the *Sunnah* (right practices) which enlighten those who seek to be directed in the right way, who is distinguished for the all-embracing wisdom of his discourse, and for his perseverance in worship of Allah. May Allah's blessing and peace be upon him, and upon the rest of the Prophets and Messengers, upon the families of them all, and upon all the believers.

It has come to us on the authority of 'Alī b. Abī Ṭālib, and 'Abdullāh b. Mas'ūd, and Mu'ādh b. Jabal, and Abū al-Dardā', and Ibn 'Umar, and Ibn 'Abbās, and Anas bin

---

[*] The Arabic text of Imam Nawawī's introduction follows immediately after this English translation.

Mālik, and Abū Hurayrah, and Abū Saʿīd al-Khudrī, all companions of the Prophet, upon whom be Allah's blessing and peace, with all of whom may Allah be pleased, through many lines of transmission, that the Messenger of Allah *sallallāhu ʿalayhi wasallam* said:

> Whoever preserves (*hafad*) for my community forty Hadīth concerning matters of this religion, Allah will on the Last Day raise him up in the company of *fuqahā* and *ʿulamā'* (jurists and scholars).

According to another line of transmission, this Hadīth reads:

> Allah will raise him up a *fāqih* and a *ʿālim*.

As transmitted by Abū al-Dardā', it reads:

> I will be an intercessor and a witness for him on the Day of Rising.

As transmitted by Ibn Masʿūd, it reads:

> It will be said to him: Enter the Garden by any Gate you please.

As transmitted by Ibn ʿUmar, it reads:

> He will be recorded in the company of the *ʿulamā'* and raised up in the company of the martyrs.

The traditional transmitters, or *muhadithūn* of Hadīth are agreed that the above is a weak tradition, even though the lines by which it has been handed down are numerous.

The *'ulamā'*—with whom may Allah be pleased—have composed innumerable works on this matter of the forty Hadīth. To my knowledge the first among them to write thereon was 'Abdullāh bin al-Mubārak. Then came Muhammad bin Aslam al-Tūsī, one who was devoted to his Lord. Then there was al-Hasan bin Sufyān al-Nasā'ī, and Abū Bakr al-Ajurrī, and Abū Bakr Muhammad bin Ibrahīm al-Isfahānī, and al-Dāraqutnī, and others too numerous to mention both among the writers of old and later. And now I have sought Allah's help in assembling forty Hadīth in imitation of these predecessors, the outstanding *muhadithūn* and scholars of Islam. The *'ulamā'* have agreed that it is permissible to make use of a weak Hadīth when it concerns a matter of praiseworthy works, yet in spite of this I have not relied on the (above recorded) Hadīth, but rather on the saying of the Prophet *sallallāhu 'alayhi wasallam* in the genuine Hadīth:

Let him among you who (was present and) saw, inform him who was absent,

and on his saying:

May Allah brighten life for any man who hears what I say, pays heed to it, and passes it on just as he heard it.

Among the *'ulamā'* are some who have assembled forty Hadīth concerning the principles of religion (*usūl al-dīn*), while others (have made their collection) with reference to the derivative matters of religion (*furū'*). Some (have made collections of forty Hadīth) about (the matter of) *jihād,* or struggle in the cause of Religion, some about ascetic practices, some about rules of conduct, others about practical discourse. All these are righteous purposes, so may Allah be pleased with such as have purposed them. My thought, however, was to compile forty Hadīth more important than any of these, viz. forty Hadīth which would include all the above mentioned—each Hadīth of which would set forth one of the fundamental points of religious belief. I will choose such Hadīth as those which the *'ulamā'* have referred to as "the pivot of Islam", or "the half of Islam", or "the third thereof", or some such title. Then I will insist that each of the forty be a "genuine" Hadīth, for the most part such as will be found in the *Sahīhayn* (two genuine books) of al-Bukhārī and of Muslim. I will record them without the *isnād*s in order to make it easier to memorise them and to make them more generally profitable—if Allah wills.

Everyone who is eager to attain the next world *(ākhirah)* ought to know these Hadīths because of the important matters they contain and the indications they give of all things in which obedience to Allah is necessary. This will be apparent to anyone who reflects on the matter. On Allah is my reliance, and He is my trust and stay. His is the praise and the worship, and with Him is success and protection.

بِسْمِ اللهِ الرَّحْمٰنِ الرَّحِيمِ

الحمد لله رب العالمين ، قيوم السموات والأرضين ،
مدبر الخلائق أجمعين ، باعث الرسل صلوات الله وسلامه عليهم
أجمعين إلى المكلفين ، لهدايتهم وبيان شرائع الدين ، بالدلائل
القطعية وواضحات البراهين . أحمده على جميع نعمه وأسأله
المزيد من فضله وكرمه . وأشهد أن لا إله إلا الله وحده لا
شريك له الواحد القهار . الكريم الغفار . وأشهد أن سيدنا
محمداً عبده ورسوله ، وحبيبه وخليله ، أفضل المخلوقين ،
المكرّم بالقرآن العزيز المعجزة المستمرّة على تعاقب السنين ،
وبالسنن المستنيرة للمسترشدين ، سيدنا محمد ، المخصوص
بجوامع الكلم وسماحة الدين . صلوات الله وسلامه عليه وعلى
سائر النبيين والمرسلين ، وآل كلّ وسائر الصالحين .

أما بعد فقد روينا عن علي بن أبي طالب وعبدالله بن
مسعود ومعاذ بن جبل وأبي الدرداء وابن عمر وابن عباس
وأنس بن مالك   وأبي هريرة   وأبي سعيد الخدري رضي
الله عنهم ، من طرق كثيرات بروايات متنوعة ، أن رسول
الله صلى الله عليه وسلم قال : « من حفظ على أمتي أربعين
حديثاً من أمر دينها بعثه الله يوم القيامة في زمرة الفقهاء والعلماء ».
وفي رواية « بعثه الله فقيهاً عالماً » ، وفي رواية أبي الدرداء « وكنت
له يوم القيامة شافعاً وشهيداً » ، وفي رواية ابن مسعود « قيل له :

ادخل من أيّ أبواب الجنة شئت » ، وفي رواية ابن عمر
« كُتِبَ في زمرة العلماء ، وحُشرَ في زمرة الشهداء » . واتفق
الحفاظ على أنه حديث ضعيف وإن كَثُرَت طرقه .

وقد صنف العلماء رضي الله عنهم في هذا الباب ما لا يحصى
من المصنفات . فأول من علمته صنف فيه عبدالله بن المبارك ،
ثم ابن أسلم الطوسي العالم الرّباني ، ثم الحسن بن سفيان
النسائي ، وأبو بكر الآجري ، وأبو بكر محمد بن إبراهيم
الأصفهاني ، والدارقطني ، والحاكم ، وأبو نُعيم ، وأبو عبد
الرحمن السُّلمي ، وأبو سعيد الماليني ، وأبو عثمان الصابوني ،
وعبدالله بن محمد الأنصاري ، وأبو بكر البيهقي . وخلائق
لا يحصون من المتقدمين والمتأخرين .

وقد استخرت الله تعالى في جمع أربعين حديثاً ، اقتداء
بهؤلاء الأئمة الأعلام وحفّاظ الإسلام . وقد اتفق العلماء على
جواز العمل بالحديث الضعيف في فضائل الأعمال . ومع هذا
فليس اعتمادي على هذا الحديث ، بل على قوله صلى الله عليه
وسلم في الأحاديث الصحيحة : « ليبلِّغْ الشاهدُ منكم الغائب » .
وقوله صلى الله عليه وسلم : « نضرَّ الله امرأً سمع مقالتي
فوعاها فأداها كما سمعها » . ثم من العلماء من جمع الأربعين
في أصول الدين ، وبعضهم في الفروع ، وبعضهم في الجهاد ،
وبعضهم في الزهد ، وبعضهم في الآداب ، وبعضهم في الخطب ،
وكلها مقاصد صالحة رضي الله عن قاصديها . وقد رأيت
جمع أربعين أهمّ من هذا كله . وهي أربعون حديثاً مشتملة

ذلك ، وكل حديث منها قاعدة عظيمة من قواعد الدين ، قد وصفه العلماء بأن مدار الإسلام عليه ، أو هو نصف الإسلام أو ثلثه أو نحو ذلك . ثم ألتزم في هذه الأربعين أن تكون صحيحة ، ومعظمها في صحيحي البخاري ومسلم ، وأذكرها محذوفة الأسانيد ليسهل حفظها ويعم الانتفاع بها إن شاء الله تعالى ، ثم أتبعها بباب في ضبط خفيّ ألفاظها .

وينبغي لكل راغب في الآخرة أن يعرف هذه الأحاديث لما اشتملت عليه من المهمات واحتوت عليه من التنبيه على جميع الطاعات ، وذلك ظاهر لمن تدبره . وعلى الله اعتمادي ، وإليه تفويضي واستنادي ، وله الحمد والنعمة ، وبه التوفيق والعصمة .

اَلْحَدِيثُ الْأَوَّلُ

عَنْ أَمِيرِ الْمُؤْمِنِينَ أَبِيْ حَفْصٍ عُمَرَ ابْنِ الْخَطَّابِ رَضِيَ اللهُ عَنْهُ قَالَ، سَمِعْتُ رَسُوْلَ اللهِ صَلَّى اللهُ عَلَيْهِ وَسَلَّمَ يَقُوْلُ: إِنَّمَا الْأَعْمَالُ بِالنِّيَّاتِ وَإِنَّمَا لِكُلِّ امْرِىءٍ مَانَوَى فَمَنْ كَانَتْ هِجْرَتُهُ إِلَى اللهِ وَرَسُوْلِهِ فَهِجْرَتُهُ إِلَى اللهِ وَرَسُوْلِهِ وَمَنْ كَانَتْ هِجْرَتُهُ لِدُنْيَا يُصِيْبُهَا أَوِامْرَأَةٍ يَنْكِحُهَا فَهِجْرَتُهُ إِلَى مَاهَاجَرَ إِلَيْهِ. رَوَاهُ إِمَامَا الْمُحَدِّثِيْنَ أَبُوْ عَبْدِ اللهِ مُحَمَّدُ بْنُ إِسْمَاعِيْلَ بْنِ إِبْرَاهِيْمَ بْنِ الْمُغِيْرَةِ ابْنِ بَرْدِزْبَهَ الْبُخَارِيُّ وَأَبُو الْحُسَيْنِ مُسْلِمُ بْنُ الْحَجَّاجِ بْنِ مُسْلِمٍ الْقُشَيْرِيُّ النَّيْسَابُوْرِيُّ فِيْ صَحِيْحَيْهِمَا اللَّذَيْنِ هُمَا أَصَحُّ الْكُتُبِ الْمُصَنَّفَةِ.

Translation:

It is narrated on the authority of Amīrul Mu'minīn, Abū Hafs 'Umar bin al-Khaṭṭāb (*radiyallāhu 'anhu*) who said: I heard the Messenger of Allah (*sallallāhu 'alayhi wasallam*) say, "Actions are (judged) by motives (*niyyāt*), so each man will have what he intended.[1] Thus, he whose migration (*hijrah*) was to Allah and His Messenger, his migration is to Allah and His Messenger; but he whose migration was for some worldly thing he might gain, or for a wife he might marry, his migration is to that for which he migrated."[2]

[Both al-Bukhārī and Muslim relate this in their books, the two *Sahīhs*, which are the soundest of the *Musannaf*s (Collections of Hadīth).]

Notes:

1.   Allah accepts our intentions, as is said in the Qur'an: *It is not their meat nor their blood, that reaches Allah, it is your piety that reaches Him* (22:37). And again: *To any that desires the tilth of the Hereafter, We give increase in his tilth; and to any that desires tilth of this world, We grant somewhat thereof, but he has no share or lot in the Hereafter* (42:20).

2.   This was uttered by the holy Prophet *sallallāhu 'alayhi wasallam* at the time when a man emigrated to Madīnah to seek the hand of a maiden, Umm e-Qays by name, but not for the sake of the religion of Islam.

عَنْ عُمَرَ رَضِيَ اللهُ عَنْهُ أَيْضًا قَالَ : بَيْنَـمَا نَحْنُ
جُلُوْسٌ عِنْدَ رَسُوْلِ اللهِ صَلَّى اللهُ عَلَيْهِ وَسَلَّمَ ذَاتَ يَوْمٍ إِذْ
طَلَعَ عَلَيْنَا رَجُلٌ شَدِيْدُ بَيَاضِ الثِّيَابِ شَدِيْدُ سَوَادِ الشَّعْرِ
لَايُرَى عَلَيْهِ أَثَرُ السَّفَرِ وَلَايَعْرِفُهُ مِنَّا أَحَدٌ حَتَّى جَلَسَ إِلَى
النَّبِيِّ صَلَّى اللهُ عَلَيْهِ وَسَلَّمَ فَأَسْنَدَ رُكْبَتَيْهِ إِلَى رُكْبَتَيْهِ
وَوَضَعَ كَفَّيْهِ عَلَى فَخِذَيْهِ وَقَالَ : يَامُحَمَّدُ أَخْبِرْنِيْ عَنِ
الْإِسْلَامِ ، فَقَالَ رَسُوْلُ اللهِ صَلَّى اللهُ عَلَيْهِ وَسَلَّمَ :
اَلْإِسْلَامُ أَنْ تَشْهَدَ أَنْ لَاإِلهَ إِلَّا اللهُ وَأَنَّ مُحَمَّدًا رَسُوْلُ اللهِ ،
وَتُقِيْمَ الصَّلَاةَ ، وَتُؤْتِيَ الزَّكَاةَ ، وَتَصُوْمَ رَمَضَانَ ، وَتَحُجَّ
الْبَيْتَ إِنِ اسْتَطَعْتَ إِلَيْهِ سَبِيْلًا . قَالَ : صَدَقْتَ فَعَجِبْنَالَهُ
يَسْأَلُهُ وَيُصَدِّقُهُ . قَالَ : فَأَخْبِرْنِيْ عَنِ الْإِيْمَانِ ، قَالَ : أَنْ
تُؤْمِنَ بِاللهِ وَمَلَائِكَتِهِ وَكُتُبِهِ وَرُسُلِهِ وَالْيَوْمِ الْآخِرِ وَتُؤْمِنَ
بِالْقَدَرِ خَيْرِهِ وَشَرِّهِ . قَالَ : صَدَقْتَ قَالَ : فَأَخْبِرْنِيْ عَنِ
الْإِحْسَانِ ، قَالَ : أَنْ تَعْبُدَ اللهَ كَأَنَّكَ تَرَاهُ فَإِنْ لَمْ تَكُنْ تَرَاهُ
فَإِنَّهُ يَرَاكَ . قَالَ : فَأَخْبِرْنِيْ عَنِ السَّاعَةِ ، قَالَ : مَاالْمَسْؤُوْلُ
عَنْهَا بِأَعْلَمَ مِنَ السَّائِلِ . قَالَ : فَأَخْبِرْنِيْ عَنْ أَمَارَاتِهَا ،

3

قَالَ : أَنْ تَلِدَ الْأَمَةُ رَبَّتَهَا وَأَنْ تَرَى الْحُفَاةَ الْعُرَاةَ الْعَالَةَ
رِعَاءَ الشَّاءِ يَتَطَاوَلُوْنَ فِي الْبُنْيَانِ ثُمَّ انْطَلَقَ فَلَبِثْتُ مَلِيًّا ثُمَّ
قَالَ : يَاعُمَرُ أَتَدْرِيْ مَنِ السَّائِلُ؟ قُلْتُ : اَللهُ وَرَسُوْلُهُ
أَعْلَمُ . قَالَ : فَإِنَّهُ جِبْرِيْلُ أَتَاكُمْ يُعَلِّمُكُمْ دِيْنَكُمْ – رَوَاهُ
مُسْلِمٌ .

Translation:

Also on the authority of 'Umar (*radiyallāhu 'anhu*) who
said: While we were one day sitting with the Messenger of
Allah *(sallallāhu 'alayhi wasallam)* there appeared before us
a man dressed in extremely white clothes and with very
black hair. No traces of journeying were visible on him, and
none of us knew him. He sat down close by the Prophet
(sallallāhu 'alayhi wasallam), rested his knees against his,
put his palms on his thighs, and said, "O Muhammad!
inform me about *Islām."* Said the Messenger of Allah
(sallallāhu 'alayhi wasallam), "Islam is that you should
testify that there is no deity save Allah and that Muhammad
is His Messenger, that you should perform *salāt* (ritual
prayer), pay the *zakāt,* fast during Ramadān, and go on Hajj
(pilgrimage) to the House (the Ka'bah at Makkah), if you
can find a way to it (or find the means for making the
journey to it)." Said he, "You have spoken truly." We were
astonished at his thus questioning him and telling that he was
right, but he went on to say, "Inform me about *Imān*
(faith)." He (the Messenger of Allah) answered, "It is that
you believe in Allah and His angels and His Books and His
Messengers and in the Last Day, and in predestination
(*qadr*), both in its good and in its evil". He said, "You have
spoken truly." Then he (the man) said, "Inform me about

4

Iḥsān". He (the Messenger of Allah) answered, "It is that you should serve Allah as though you could see Him, for though you cannot see Him yet He sees you". He said, "Inform me about the Hour". He (the Messenger of Allah) said, "About that the one questioned knows no more than the questioner." So he said, "Well, inform me about the signs thereof (i.e. of its coming)". Said he, "They are that the slave-girl will give birth to her mistress, that you will see the barefooted ones, the naked, the destitute, the herdsmen of the sheep (competing with each other) in raising lofty buildings". Thereupon the man went off. I waited a while, and then he (the Messenger of Allah) said, "O 'Umar, do you know who that was?" I replied, "Allah and His Messenger know better." He said, "That was Jibrīl. He came to teach you your religion."
[Muslim relates this.]

عَنْ أَبِيْ عَبْدِ الرَّحْمٰنِ عَبْدِ اللهِ بْنِ عُمَرَ بْنِ الْخَطَّابِ
رَضِيَ اللهُ عَنْهُمَا قَالَ: سَمِعْتُ رَسُوْلَ اللهِ صَلَّى اللهُ عَلَيْهِ
وَسَلَّمَ يَقُوْلُ: بُنِيَ الْإِسْلَامُ عَلَى خَمْسٍ: شَهَادَةِ أَنْ لَاإِلٰهَ
إِلَّا اللهُ وَأَنَّ مُحَمَّدًا رَسُوْلُ اللهِ، وَإِقَامِ الصَّلَاةِ، وَإِيْتَاءِ
الزَّكَاةِ وَحَجِّ الْبَيْتِ، وَصَوْمِ رَمَضَانَ. رَوَاهُ الْبُخَارِيُّ
وَمُسْلِمٌ.

Translation:

On the authority of Abū 'Abd al-Raḥmān 'Abdullāh bin
'Umar bin al-Khaṭṭāb (*radiyallāhu 'anhumā*)* who said: I
heard the Messenger of Allah (*ṣallallāhu 'alayhi wasallam*)
say: "Islam has been built upon five things - on testifying
that there is no god save Allah, and that Muhammad is His
Messenger; on performing *salāt* (ritual prayer); on giving the
zakāt; on Hajj to the House; and on fasting during
Ramaḍān."
[Both al-Bukhārī and Muslim relate this.]

---

* *Radiyallāhu 'anhumā* (may Allah be pleased with both of them): the invocation
is on both 'Abdullāh bin 'Umar and his revered father, 'Umar bin al-Khaṭṭāb.

‏عَنْ أَبِيْ عَبْدِ الرَّحْمٰنِ عَبْدِ اللهِ بْنِ مَسْعُوْدٍ رَضِيَ اللهُ‏
‏عَنْهُ قَالَ : حَدَّثَنَا رَسُوْلُ اللهِ صَلَّى اللهُ عَلَيْهِ وَسَلَّمَ وَهُوَ‏
‏الصَّادِقُ الْمَصْدُوْقِ . إِنَّ أَحَدَكُمْ يُجْمَعُ خَلْقُهُ فِيْ بَطْنِ أُمِّهِ‏
‏أَرْبَعِيْنَ يَوْمًا نُطْفَةً ثُمَّ يَكُوْنُ عَلَقَةً مِثْلَ ذٰلِكَ ثُمَّ يَكُوْنُ‏
‏مُضْغَةً مِثْلَ ذٰلِكَ ثُمَّ يُرْسَلُ إِلَيْهِ الْمَلَكُ فَيَنْفُخُ فِيْهِ الرُّوْحَ‏
‏وَيُؤْمَرُ بِأَرْبَعِ كَلِمَاتٍ بِكَتْبِ رِزْقِهِ وَأَجَلِهِ وَعَمَلِهِ وَشَقِيٌّ‏
‏أَوْ سَعِيْدٌ فَوَ اللهِ الَّذِيْ لَاإِلٰهَ غَيْرُهُ إِنَّ أَحَدَكُمْ لَيَعْمَلُ بِعَمَلِ‏
‏أَهْلِ الْجَنَّةِ حَتَّى مَايَكُوْنَ بَيْنَهُ وَبَيْنَهَا إِلَّا ذِرَاعٌ فَيَسْبِقُ إِلَيْهِ‏
‏الْكِتَابُ فَيَعْمَلُ بِعَمَلِ أَهْلِ النَّارِ فَيَدْخُلُهَا وَإِنَّ أَحَدَكُمْ‏
‏لَيَعْمَلُ بِعَمَلِ أَهْلِ النَّارِ حَتَّى مَايَكُوْنَ بَيْنَهُ وَبَيْنَهَا إِلَّا‏
‏ذِرَاعٌ فَيَسْبِقُ عَلَيْهِ الْكِتَابُ فَيَعْمَلُ بِعَمَلِ أَهْلِ الْجَنَّةِ‏
‏فَيَدْخُلُهَا - رَوَاهُ الْبُخَارِيُّ وَمُسْلِمٌ .‏

Translation:

Abū 'Abd al-Rahmān 'Abdullāh bin Mas'ūd (*radiyallāhu 'anhu*) reported: The Messenger of Allah (*sallallāhu 'alayhi wasallam*), the most truthful, the most trusted, told us, "Verily the creation of any one of you takes place when he is assembled in his mother's womb; for forty days he is as a drop, then he becomes a clot, in the same way, and then, in the same way, a mass. Then an angel is sent to him, who breathes the *rūh* (spirit) into him.[1] Four words of

command are given to this angel, viz. that he write down his provision (*rizq*), his life-span, his deeds, and whether he will be among the wretched or the blessed (at Judgement). By Allah - there is no deity but He - one of you may work the works of the people of the Garden till there is naught but an arm's length between him and it, when that which has been written will outstrip him so that he works the works of the people of the Fire; one of you may do the works of the people of the Fire, till there is naught but an arm's length between him and it, when that which has been written will overtake him so that he works the works of the people of the Garden and enters therein."[2]
[Both al-Bukhārī and Muslim relate this.]

Notes:

1.   The very beginning of the revelation speaks of the creative power of Allah, in particular the creation of man and his origin: *Read in the name of Thy Lord Who creates - creates man from a clot* (Qur'an 96:1).

2.   This reflects the grace and mercy of the Creator as much as it reflects His power. It is out of His grace that He has elevated this clot of blood to the rank of man, and taught him "by the pen, taught man what he knew not".

In another place the Qur'an says: *O people, if you are in doubt about the Resurrection, then surely We created you from dust, then from a small life-germ, then from a clot, then from a lump of flesh, complete in make and incomplete, that We may make clear to you. And We cause what We please to remain in the wombs till an appointed time, then We bring you forth as babies, then that you may attain your maturity. And of you is he who is caused to die, and of you is he who is brought back to the worst part of life, so that after knowledge he knows nothing. And thou seest the earth barren, but when We send down thereon water, it stirs and swells and brings forth a beautiful (growth) of every kind* (22:5).

In another verse the Qur'an says: . . . *He creates you in the wombs of your mothers - creation after creation - in triple darkness. That is Allah your Lord* (39:6). And again: *Allah is He Who made the earth a resting place for you and the heaven a structure, and He formed you, then made goodly your forms, and He provided you with goodly things. That is Allah, your Lord - so blessed is Allah, the Lord of the worlds* (40:64).

The stages of a man's physical growth from nothing till he completes the cycle of this life are described in words whose accuracy, beauty, and comprehensiveness can only be fully understood by biologists. Modern scientific research has revealed the highly complex nature of the process of conception and the subsequent stages leading up the growth of the human body. Fertilisation of the ovary or female egg with the male sperm (millions floating in the drop of semen), is the starting point of conception. The fertilised ovary plus sperm takes the scientific name of zygote and it begins to undergo a process of cell division, which would determine the sex and the physical features and mental powers of the human body. After the cell division, the zygote can be differentiated as a complex sphere. This the stage of the clot, but its shape is irregular. This stage is complete, in so far as cell division is concerned, but incomplete as full biological growth. The zygote takes about ten days to develop into embryo. The human embryo develops rather slowly, and six weeks after fertilisation it is only ⅔" long. This is referred to in the Qur'an as creation after creation. The development of the zygote to embryo, of the embryo to the foetus, and the foetus to a baby are surely stages of creation after creation, because one stage represents the completion of one process, and the second stage is so different from the previous one in its characteristics, that it can be rightly described in the manner of the Qur'an. The triple darkness perhaps would mean the three stages referred to above.

The Hadīth has described the processes in detail. The period of forty days from semen to clot, and of the clot (or embryo) for the same period, approximate with scientific research. The human embryo develops in 6 weeks (or 42 days) after fertilisation. The development of a foetus takes almost the same period, and it is after about 3 months that it takes a recognisable human form. The movement of the baby in mother's womb starts after this period. It may be noted however, that the modern scientific information about the stages in the growth of a human baby from conception to delivery, is the product of highly advanced techniques in the study of human biology. Surgical operations, drugs and X-rays have made some of this knowledge possible. But 1,400 years ago none could dream of such an analytical and specific description of the phases of human growth from conception to birth, much less from the unlettered Prophet of the Desert. This is another proof that his knowledge which is now corroborated by modern scientific research was divinely inspired.

3.   The problem of pre-destination and human independence is a very difficult and delicate matter which has challenged great minds from Socrates to Russell. No one can claim to give a true answer to this eternal riddle. However the position of Islam on pre-destination is much misunderstood and even more misrepresented. The picture of a Muslim as lazy creature of Fate or *Qismat*, so popular in the West has little relation to the truth of Islamic faith and to the reality of history, for it was with the dynamism inspired by Islam that they swept, within seventy years, from Spain in the West to Sind in the East, and created an empire which was undoubtedly the greatest cultural and civilisational achievement of history. They not only built the largest empire but also gave an intellectual lead to the world. The fatalistic in the sense of inactive is the product of Muslim decadence.

عَنْ أُمِّ الْمُؤْمِنِيْنَ أُمِّ عَبْدِ اللهِ عَائِشَةَ رَضِيَ اللهُ عَنْهَا
قَالَتْ، قَالَ رَسُوْلُ اللهِ صَلَّى اللهُ عَلَيْهِ وَسَلَّمَ : مَنْ أَحْدَثَ
فِيْ أَمْرِنَا هٰـذَا مَالَيْسَ مِنْـهُ فَهُوَ رَدٌّ – رَوَاهُ الْبُخَـارِيُّ
وَمُسْلِمٌ . وَفِيْ رِوَايَةٍ لِمُسْلِمٍ مَنْ عَمِلَ عَمَلًا لَيْسَ عَلَيْهِ
أَمْرُنَا فَهُوَ رَدٌّ .

Translation:

It is narrated on the authority of the Mother of the Believers,
Umm 'Abdullāh 'Ā'ishah (*radiyallāhu 'anhā*) that   the
Messenger of Allah (*sallallāhu 'alayhi wasallam*) said,
"Whosoever introduces into this affair of ours (i.e. into
Islam) something that does not belong to it, it is to be
rejected."
[Both al-Bukhārī and Muslim relate this.]

According to the version in Muslim, (it reads): "Whosoever
works a work which has for it no command of ours is to be
rejected."

عَنْ أَبِيْ عَبْدِ اللهِ النُّعْمَانِ بْنِ بَشِيْرٍ رَضِيَ اللهُ عَنْهُمَا
قَالَ: سَمِعْتُ رَسُوْلَ اللهِ صَلَّى اللهُ عَلَيْهِ وَسَلَّمَ يَقُوْلُ: إِنَّ
الْحَلَالَ بَيِّنٌ وَإِنَّ الْحَرَامَ بَيِّنٌ وَبَيْنَهُمَا أُمُوْرٌ مُشْتَبِهَاتٌ
لَايَعْلَمُهُنَّ كَثِيْرٌ مِنَ النَّاسِ فَمَنِ اتَّقَى الشُّبُهَاتِ فَقَدِ
اسْتَبْرَأَ لِدِيْنِهِ وَعِرْضِهِ وَمَنْ وَقَعَ فِي الشُّبُهَاتِ وَقَعَ فِي
الْحَرَامِ كَالرَّاعِيْ يَرْعَى حَوْلَ الْحِمَى يُوْشِكُ أَنْ يَرْتَعَ فِيْهِ
أَلَا وَإِنَّ لِكُلِّ مَلِكٍ حِمًى أَلَا وَإِنَّ حِمَى اللهِ مَحَارِمُهُ أَلَا وَإِنَّ
فِي الْجَسَدِ مُضْغَةً إِذَا صَلَحَتْ صَلَحَ الْجَسَدُ كُلُّهُ وَإِذَا
فَسَدَتْ فَسَدَ الْجَسَدُ كُلُّهُ أَلَا وَهِيَ الْقَلْبُ - رَوَاهُ
الْبُخَارِيُّ وَمُسْلِمٌ.

Translation:

On the authority of Abū 'Abdullāh al-Nu'mān bin Bashīr (*radiyallāhu 'anhumā*) who said: I heard the Messenger of Allah (*sallallāhu 'alayhi wasallam*) say, "Truly, what is lawful is evident, and what is unlawful is evident, and in between the two are matters which are doubtful which many people do not know. He who guards against doubtful things keeps his religion and honour blameless, and he who indulges in doubtful things indulges in fact in unlawful things, just as a shepherd who pastures his flock round a preserve will soon pasture them in it. Beware, every king has a preserve, and the things God has declared unlawful are His preserves.[1] Beware, in the body there is a piece of flesh; if it is sound, the whole body is sound, and if it is corrupt, the whole body is corrupt, and behold, it is the heart."

[Both al-Bukhārī and Muslim relate this.]

Note:

1. Islam lays down the laws clearly and forcefully but does not work out details of the applications of the laws in different cases and situations, which was done by great jurists like Imam Abū Ḥanīfah, Imam Mālik, Imam al-Shāfi'ī and Imam Aḥmad bin Ḥanbal. The differences between these great scholars are on shades of emphasis and points of interpretation. All of them agreed on the fundamentals which define the lawful and unlawful. It is lawful, for example, for a man to divorce and even for a woman to obtain divorce, but if this lawful right is exercised in an irresponsible and immoral fashion, it could lead unto injustice and sin. So there are many undesirable attitudes and actions, between the lawful and the unlawful, which must be scrupulously avoided for fear of erring into sin.

Hadīth 7

اَلْحَدِيْثُ السَّابِعُ

عَنْ أَبِيْ رُقَيَّةَ تَمِيْمِ بْنِ أَوْسٍ الدَّارِيِّ رَضِيَ اللهُ عَنْهُ
أَنَّ النَّبِيَّ صَلَّى اللهُ عَلَيْهِ وَسَلَّمَ قَالَ : اَلدِّيْنُ النَّصِيْحَةُ قُلْنَا
لِمَنْ؟ قَـالَ : لِلّهِ وَلِكِتَابِهِ وَلِرَسُوْلِهِ وَلِأَئِمَّةِ الْمُسْلِمِيْنَ
وَعَامَّتِهِمْ - رَوَاهُ مُسْلِمٌ .

Translation:

It is narrated on the authority of Abū Ruqayyah Tamīm bin Aus al-Dārī (*radiyallāhu 'anhu*) that the Prophet (*sallallāhu 'alayhi wasallam*) said, "Religion is *nasīhah*".[1] (Upon this) we said, "For whom?" and he answered, "for Allah,[2] for His Book,[3] for His Messenger,[4] and for the Imams of the Muslims,[5] and the generality of them".[6]

[Muslim relates this.]

Notes:

1.   The word *nasīhah* is derived from the verb *nasaha* which carries a wide range of meanings: to give (someone) sincere advise, advise, counsel (someone to do something), admonish, exhort; to be sincere, to mean well, wish someone well, be well-disposed, show good will, to act in good faith, to give sincere advise, to be sincere in one's intentions towards someone; to be loyal and sincere to each other; to take good advice, follow an advice, etc.   Imam Abū Sulaymān Khaṭṭabī says: It is a very comprehensive term and it stands for all those virtues and deeds for which the counsel is given. Some are of the opinion that it originally means to 'sew the garment or to purify the honey' as we have such expression in Arabic as *nasaha al-rajulu thawbatan*,

14

nasahat al-'asal. Thus according to its derivation it would mean to make man's heart chaste and pure and to order his life according to Islam with sincere counsel or advice. *Nasīhah* is the opposite of impurity and alloy.

2. In the light of these meanings the *nasīhah* for Allah would imply that man's heart is cleansed from all impurities and alloys with regard to belief in Allah, i.e. one should believe in Him as the Sole Creator and Master with all His attributes and with an earnest desire to obey all commands given by Him.

3. *Nasīhah* in the case of Allah's Book means that it should be sincerely believed as a revelation from the Lord and should be read and understood with the same zeal and enthusiasm in which the Divine Message is read, and all its commands must be carried out in a spirit of devotion.

4. *Nasīhah* for the Messenger signifies that his Apostlehood must be affirmed with perfect sincerity of heart and whatever he has vouchsafed to humanity should be respected as the Word and Will of God and he should be respectfully followed in all his precepts and examples and obeyed in all the commands given by him.

5. *Nasīhah* for the leaders and rulers implies that they should be respected, obeyed and given support in all those affairs which they conduct according to the *Sharī'ah* of Islam. But where they deviate from the path of righteousness they should be advised and admonished and sincere efforts be made to bring them to the right path.

6. *Nasīhah* for the general Muslims is that they should be advised in all matters concerning the good of this world and the hereafter, their life, honour and dignity should be protected and sincere endeavour made to ameliorate their lot.

Nasīhah thus cover the whole field of religion and its scope is as wide as that of Islam itself. It applies both to words and deeds. It is a *fard al-kifāyah*.

عَنِ ابْنِ عُمَرَ رَضِيَ اللهُ عَنْهُمَا أَنَّ رَسُوْلَ اللهِ صَلَّى اللهُ
عَلَيْهِ وَسَلَّمَ قَالَ : أُمِرْتُ أَنْ أُقَاتِلَ النَّاسَ حَتَّى يَشْهَدُوْا أَنْ
لاَإِلٰهَ إِلاَّ اللهُ وَأَنَّ مُحَمَّدًا رَسُوْلُ اللهِ وَيُقِيْمُوْا الصَّلاَةَ
وَيُؤْتُوْا الزَّكَاةَ. فَإِذَا فَعَلُوْا ذٰلِكَ عَصَمُوْا مِنِّي دِمَاءَهُمْ
وَأَمْوَالَهُمْ إِلاَّ بِحَقِّ الْإِسْلاَمِ وَحِسَابُهُمْ عَلَى اللهِ تَعَالَى –
رَوَاهُ الْبُخَارِيُّ وَمُسْلِمٌ .

Translation:

Ibn 'Umar (*radiyallāhu 'anhumā*) reported that the Messenger of Allah (*sallallāhu 'alayhi wasallam*) said,"I have been commanded to wage war[1] on the people till they testify that there is no deity save Allah, and that Muhammad is the Messenger of Allah, (till they) establish *salāt* (the regular prayers)[2] and give the *zakāt*. If they do that they have preserved their blood and their property from me, save that to which Islam has a right, and their reckoning is with Allah, exalted be He."
[Both al-Bukhārī and Muslim relate this.]

Notes:

1.   The sword is to be used for correction and protection and not for aggression and exploitation. There is perpetual conflict between the forces of good and evil, and the Muslim is required to fight against such evil forces until good triumphs. Islam is a world revolutionary movement to establish peace and justice, the very

17

purpose for which the prophets were sent by God. *Certainly, We sent our Messengers with clear arguments, and sent down with them the Book and the Balance, so that men may conduct themselves with justice* (Qur'an 57:25). There are numerous verses in the Qur'an exhorting the believers to fight to establish justice.

2. The five canonical prayers are meant here, and not just prayer in the ordinary sense in English.

عَنْ أَبِيْ هُرَيْرَةَ عَبْدِ الرَّحْمٰنِ بْنِ صَخْرٍ رَضِيَ اللهُ عَنْهُ
قَالَ: سَمِعْتُ رَسُوْلَ اللهِ صَلَّى اللهُ عَلَيْهِ وَسَلَّمَ يَقُوْلُ:
مَانَهَيْتُكُمْ عَنْهُ فَاجْتَنِبُوْهُ وَمَاأَمَرْتُكُمْ بِهِ فَأْتُوْا مِنْهُ
مَااسْتَطَعْتُمْ فَإِنَّمَا أَهْلَكَ الَّذِيْنَ مِنْ قَبْلِكُمْ كَثْرَةُ مَسَائِلِهِمْ
وَاخْتِلَافِهِمْ عَلَى أَنْبِيَائِهِمْ - رَوَاهُ الْبُخَارِيُّ وَمُسْلِمٌ.

Translation:

Abū Hurayrah 'Abd al-Rahmān bin Ṣakhr (*radiyallāhu 'anhu*) reported: I heard the Messenger of Allah (*sallallāhu 'alayhi wasallam*) say, "What I have declared forbidden to you, avoid; what I have bidden you do, comply with as far as you are able. What destroyed those (peoples) who were before you was naught but the number of their questionings and their disagreements with their Prophets."
[Both al-Bukhārī and Muslim relate this.]

19

عَنْ أَبِيْ هُرَيْرَةَ رَضِيَ اللهُ عَنْهُ قَالَ ، قَالَ رَسُوْلُ اللهِ

صَلَّى اللهُ عَلَيْهِ وَسَلَّمَ : إِنَّ اللهَ تَعَالَى طَيِّبٌ لَايَقْبَلُ إِلَّا طَيِّبًا

وَإِنَّ اللهَ أَمَرَ الْمُؤْمِنِيْنَ بِمَاأَمَرَ بِهِ الْمُرْسَلِيْنَ فَقَالَ تَعَالَى : يَأَيُّهَا

الرُّسُلُ كُلُوْا مِنَ الطَّيِّبَاتِ وَاعْمَلُوْا صَالِحًا ، وَقَالَ تَعَالَى :

يَأَيُّهَا الَّذِيْنَ آمَنُوْا كُلُوْا مِنْ طَيِّبَاتِ مَارَزَقْنَاكُمْ . ثُمَّ ذَكَرَ

الرَّجُلُ يُطِيْلُ السَّفَرَ أَشْعَثَ أَغْبَرَ يَمُدُّ يَدَيْهِ إِلَى السَّمَاءِ :

يَارَبُّ يَارَبُّ . وَمَطْعَمُهُ حَرَامٌ وَمَشْرَبُهُ حَرَامٌ وَمَلْبَسُهُ

حَرَامٌ وَغُذِيَ بِالْحَرَامِ فَأَنَّى يُسْتَجَابُ لَهُ - رَوَاهُ مُسْلِمٌ .

Translation:

It is narrated on the authority of Abū Hurayrah (*radiyallāhu 'anhu*) that the Messenger of Allah (*sallallāhu 'alayhi wasallam*) said, "Truly Allah is pure. He does not accept but what is pure. Allah commands the believers with what he commanded the Messengers. He has said: *O you Messengers, eat of the good things and act righteously* (Qur'an, 23:51-53); and He has also said: *O you who believe, eat of the good things which We have provided for you* (2:167-172)." Then the Prophet mentioned (the case of) the man who lengthens out his journey, who is dishevelled and dusty, but who stretches out his hands to heaven (saying), 'O Lord! O Lord!' (while) his food was unlawful, his drink was unlawful, his clothing was unlawful, and he is

nourished with unlawful things, how can he be responded to for that?"[1]
[Muslim relates this.]

Note:

1. Prayer is accepted upon two conditions: if a man is truthful and if he is clothed and nourished by lawful and pure things. Earnest prayer of a man in journeys, such as on pilgrimage, for acquisition of learning etc., is accepted provided he observes the former two conditions. As light and darkness cannot live together, so purity and impurity, cleanliness or uncleanliness cannot live together. Allah is pure and He loves purity of men. If a lawful and unlawful things are not observed, there is then no distinction between men and lower animals. Animals take grass from whichever field they get it. They can't have any sense of distinction. So also men who have got no sense of ownership. Such is the time in which we live. The only motto of the present world is to achieve object by any means, fair or foul.

Hadīth 11

اَلْحَدِيثُ الْحَادِي عَشَرَ

عَنْ أَبِي مُحَمَّدٍ الْحَسَنِ بْنِ عَلِيِّ بْنِ أَبِي طَالِبٍ سِبْطِ رَسُوْلِ اللهِ صَلَّى اللهُ عَلَيْهِ وَسَلَّمَ وَرَيْحَانَتِهِ رَضِيَ اللهُ عَنْهُمَا قَالَ، حَفِظْتُ مِنْ رَسُوْلِ اللهِ صَلَّى اللهُ عَلَيْهِ وَسَلَّمَ: دَعْ مَايَرِيْبُكَ إِلَى مَالاَ يَرِيْبُكَ. رَوَاهُ التِّرْمِذِيُّ وَالنَّسَائِيُّ، وَقَالَ التِّرْمِذِيُّ: حَدِيْثٌ حَسَنٌ صَحِيْحٌ.

Translation:

On the authority of Abū Muhammad al-Hasan bin 'Alī bin Abī Tālib, the grandson[1] of the Messenger of Allah (*sallallāhu 'alayhi wasallam*) and who are dearest to him[2] (*radiyallāhu 'anhumā*) who said: I committed to memory from the Messenger of Allah (*sallallāhu 'alayhi wasallam*) (the following words): Leave that about which you are in doubt for that about which you are in no doubt.[3]

[Al-Tirmidhī and al-Nasā'ī related it, and al-Tirmidhī said: It is a good and genuine Hadīth.]

Notes:

1. *Sibt* means grandson, but in common usage signifies 'daughter's son', distinguished by them from *hafīd* which they apply to son's children. *Sibt, sibtāni* and *asbāt* also signify the 'particularly distinguished', and 'choicest', of children. Thus it is said that *al-Hasan wa'l-Husayn sibtā Rasūlillāh*, (al-Hasan and al-Husayn are the two grandsons of the Messenger of Allah). (Lane's *English Arabic Lexicon*, p.1204.)

2. The word *rayḥānatihi* literally means 'his aromas' (perfumes), suggesting his intense love for his grandsons.

3. The broad categories of behaviour and common situations were analysed by the jurists but that did not exclude the existence of problems which could put a person in doubt regarding the lawfulness of a course of action. The habit of smoking, for example, could be cited as exceptional situation. Some *ulama* considered smoking as a wasteful and harmful practice repugnant to the Islamic spirit of cleanliness. However other *ulama* were willing to tolerate smoking as a harmless nuisance like the smell of garlic or onions which should be avoided before going to masjids for fear of causing offence to other worshippers. In Iran this problem took a political turn in late 19th century. The Shi'ī *ulama* decreed smoking to be un-Islamic in order to fight against the British strangle-hold on Iranian economy. This wide divergence of opinions, however inconsequential from the religious point of view, is likely to baffle a person and create doubts. In such predicament a Muslim is advised to follow the counsel of his heart and avoid course of action which upsets him. This advice is significant for another reason also. Islam postulates human nature to be basically good and the inherent good of man would prevail in situations of doubt and save him from falling into sin and error. The innate good symbolised by conscience is the best guide when doubt assail a person regarding problems which are not fundamental but of peripheral nature. (*see also Ḥadīth 6*)

عَنْ أَبِيْ هُرَيْرَةَ رَضِيَ اللهُ عَنْهُ قَالَ، قَالَ رَسُوْلُ اللهِ
صَلَّى اللهُ عَلَيْهِ وَسَلَّمَ : مِنْ حُسْنِ اِسْلَامِ الْمَرْءِ تَرْكُهُ مَالَا
يَعْنِيْهِ . حَدِيْثٌ حَسَنٌ . رَوَاهُ التِّرْمِذِيُّ وَغَيْرُهُ هٰكَذَا .

Translation:

On the authority of Abū Hurayrah (*radiyallāhu 'anhu*) who said: The Messenger of Allah (*sallallāhu 'alayhi wasallam*) said, "(Part of) the beauty of a man's Islam, is that he leaves alone things which are no concern of his."[1]
[A good Tradition. Al-Tirmidhī relates this and others related it also like this.]

Note:

1. This Hadīth is not a prescription to be self-centred or be selfish. A Muslim who does not concern himself with the affair of the *Ummah* is not a Muslim, says a Hadīth. This Hadīth is about the social conduct of a Muslim. A Muslim is expected to be a gentleman in every sense of the word. It is a well-known fact, that nothing poisons mutual relations between individuals more than interference in others affairs. Unhealthy curiosity, prying and eavesdropping, backbiting, scandal mongering and character assassination are some of the common forms of unwanted concern for the affairs of others. A refined religious man should abandon them and spend his time in helping his fellowmen without being a nuisance to others. *See also Hadīth 13.*

Hadīth 13

اَلْحَدِيْثُ الثَّالِثَ عَشَرَ

عَنْ أَبِيْ حَمْزَةَ أَنَسِ بْنِ مَالِكٍ رَضِيَ اللهُ عَنْهُ خَادِمِ
رَسُوْلِ اللهِ صَلَّى اللهُ عَلَيْهِ وَسَلَّمَ عَنِ النَّبِيِّ صَلَّى اللهُ عَلَيْهِ
وَسَلَّمَ قَالَ : لَا يُؤْمِنُ أَحَدُكُمْ حَتَّى يُحِبَّ لِأَخِيْهِ مَايُحِبُّ
لِنَفْسِهِ – رَوَاهُ الْبُخَارِيُّ وَمُسْلِمٌ .

Translation:

Abū Ḥamzah Anas bin Mālik (*radiyallāhu 'anhu*) who was the servant of the Messenger of Allah (*sallallāhu 'alayhi wasallam*) reported that the Prophet (*sallallāhu 'alayhi wasallam*) said, "No one of you (really) believes in (Allah and in His religion) until he loves for his brother what he loves for his own self."
[Al-Bukhārī and Muslim relate this.]

عَنِ ابْنِ مَسْعُوْدٍ رَضِيَ اللهُ عَنْهُ قَالَ ، قَالَ رَسُوْلُ اللهِ
صَـلَّى اللهُ عَلَيْهِ وَسَلَّمَ : لَايَحِـلُّ دَمُ امْرِىءٍ مُسْلِمٍ إِلَّا
بِإِحْدَى ثَلَاثٍ : اَلثَّيِّبُ الـزَّانِيْ ، وَالنَّفْسُ بِـالنَّفْسِ ،
وَالتَّارِكُ لِدِيْنِهِ الْمُفَارِقُ لِلْجَمَاعَةِ - رَوَاهُ الْبُخَارِيُّ
وَمُسْلِمٌ .

Translation:

On the authority of Ibn Mas'ūd (*radiyallāhu 'anhu*) who
said: The Messenger of Allah (*sallallāhu 'alayhi wasallam*)
said, "The blood of a man who is a Muslim is not lawful
(i.e. cannot be lawfully shed), save if he belongs to one of
three (classes): a married man who is an adulterer;[1] life for
a life (i.e. for murder); one who is a deserter of his
religion, abandoning the community (*jamā'ah*)".[2]
[Both al-Bukhārī and Muslim relate this.]

Notes:

1.   Chastity, as a virtue, is not given the first place in modern
civilised society, and hence adultery is not considered a sufficiently
serious offence to subject the guilty party to any punishment except
the payment of damages to the injured husband (or a small fine by
the *Sharī'ah* court). The breach of the greatest trust which can be
imposed in a man or a woman, the breach which ruins families,
destroys household peace, and deprives innocent children of their
loving mothers, is not looked upon even as seriously as the breach

26

of trust of a few dollars. Hence Islamic law seems to be too severe to a Westerner or Western mind.

The punishment for adultery in this Hadīth is stated to be death, not flogging which was prescribed by the Qur'an (24:2, *and also see* Qur'an, 4:25: where in the case of slave girls: . . . *then, if they are guilty of adultery when they are taken in marriage, they shall suffer half the punishment for free married women.* Volumes have been written on the 'right' punishment for adultery in Islamic criminal law and the controversy whether 'stoning' is in fact the punishment prescribed in the Qur'an for adultery has taken a new significance in view of the total absence of a moral environment in the modern world, and the social change that is taking place consequent upon uninhibited glorification of sex and violence through the global electronic and print media. The concession made in the case of a slave girl probably is due to the fact that her weaker social status of a slave makes her, obviously, more accessible to temptation than a free married woman is presumed to be. In the modern world where corruption and immorality are global, a Muslim is exposed to too many temptations than he would be if he lives in an Islamic environment under a truly Islamic government. Muslim jurists should find a practical solution to this problem and such other problems in the light of the Qur'an and true spirit of Sunnah through *ijtihād*.

For further reading please see *Sahīh Muslim* translated by Abdul Hamid Siddiqui, p.898, note 2131; *Islamic Jurisprudence in the Modern World* by A.A.Qadri, p.296; *The Religion of Islam* by Muḥammad 'Alī, p.752; commentaries on the relevant verses in *The Holy Qur'ān* by Muhammad Asad, 'Abdullāh Yūsuf 'Alī, Muḥammad 'Alī, and others.

2. Abdul Hamid Siddiqui comments: Apostasy in Islam implies deliberate abandonment of Islam. There is almost consensus of opinion amongst the jurists that apostasy from Islam (*Irtidād*) must be punished with death.

The apostate is not immediately put to death but is given a fair chance to explain his viewpoint and every effort is made to convince him of the foolishness of this act of his and bring him to repentance. The Hanafites are inclined to think that the punishment of death on account of apostasy is applicable to men. According to them, women are only to be kept in prison until they repent, because the Holy Prophet *ṣallallāhu 'alayhi wasallam* has forbidden the putting to death of unbelieving women. Those who differ with this view assert that this had reference only to the killing of the unbelieving women in war and not the apostate women.

There has been a good deal of criticism against the severe punishment which Islam prescribes for apostasy. The main line of argument is that acceptance and abandonment of religion is a matter of one's own choice and should not, therefore, be made cognizable offence. This whole argument is based on one wrong supposition and that is the reason why the punishment prescribed by Islam for apostasy seem to be tyrannical. If Islam were a mere religion in the sense in which this term is commonly used, a hotchpotch of dogmas and rituals, having no direct relation with the economic, political and social structure of society, then such severe punishment of apostasy would have certainly been the height of high-handedness because the change of religion would not have, in the least, disturbed the social order. But the problem is that in Islam the Kingdom of Heaven whose foundations are firstly laid in the heart of man is to be essentially externalised in every phase of social set up, i.e. in politics, in economics, in law, in manners and in international relations. In such circumstances it is quite obvious that when a person rebels against the Kingdom of Heaven within his heart, he commits high treason against the Kingdom of Heaven on earth, the visible and concrete expression of the Kingdom of Heaven within the heart. The person who commits treason are always dealt with severely in every political order. No clemency is shown to them who undermine the foundations of the State and disrupt the social order. A stern attitude is always adopted by all sane governments against rebels and disruptionists, and so is the case with Islam. There is nothing unusual about what Islam has done. If one cares to reflect deeply over the words of the *ahādīth* one would find that there is implied reference to this aspect of the problem. The words are "The abandoner of his religion and the deserter of the society." These words imply that in Islam religion is not a matter of private

28

relations between man and God, but is intertwined with society. So when one abandons Islam he in fact revolts against the authority of the Islamic State and society (*Sahīh Muslim, English translation* vol.III, page 899, note 2132).

عَنْ أَبِيْ هُرَيْرَةَ رَضِيَ اللهُ عَنْهُ أَنَّ رَسُوْلَ اللهِ صَلَّى اللهُ
عَلَيْهِ وَسَلَّمَ قَالَ : مَنْ كَانَ يُؤْمِنُ بِاللهِ وَالْيَوْمِ الْآخِرِ فَلْيَقُلْ
خَيْرًا أَوْ لِيَصْمُتْ، وَمَنْ كَانَ يُؤْمِنُ بِاللهِ وَالْيَوْمِ الْآخِرِ
فَلْيُكْرِمْ جَارَهُ، وَمَنْ كَانَ يُؤْمِنُ بِاللهِ وَالْيَوْمِ الْآخِرِ فَلْيُكْرِمْ
ضَيْفَهُ . رَوَاهُ الْبُخَارِيُّ وَمُسْلِمٌ .

Translation:

Abū Hurayrah (*radiyallāhu 'anhu*) reported that the Messenger of Allah (*sallallāhu 'alayhi wasallam*) said, "Let whosoever believes in Allah and in the Last Day either speak good or be silent. Let whosoever believes in Allah and in the Last Day honour his neighbour. Let whosoever believes in Allah and in the Last Day honour his guest."[1]
[Both al-Bukhārī and Muslim relate it.]

Note:

1.   The Prophet *sallallāhu 'alayhi wasallam* stressed these points in a number of other sayings. "A *Muslim* is he from whose tongue and hand people are safe, and *Mu'min* is he who could be trusted by the people for their lives and wealth" (Related by Muslim, *see Kitāb al-Imān, Mishkāt al-Masābih*). Prophet *sallallāhu 'alayhi wasallam* loved his neighbours, helped them and even worked for them with his own hands. So great was the emphasis laid by the Holy Prophet on the right of neighbour that the companions began to feel that neighbours would also be made rightful heirs to the property of a deceased. History is replete with examples which

illustrate the generosity of Muslims to the guests and neighbours. Sultan Salahuddin treated King Richard as a guest in his land, and for that reason he sent him medical aid and fruits during Richard's illness although Richard was responsible for the savage murder of 2,700 Muslims of Acre. These two qualities inculcated by the Prophet by precept and practice became the basis of Muslim chivalry in the Middle Ages.

Hadīth 16

اَلْحَدِيْثُ السَّادِسَ عَشَرَ

عَنْ أَبِيْ هُرَيْرَةَ رَضِيَ اللهُ عَنْهُ أَنَّ رَجُلاً قَالَ لِلنَّبِيِّ
صَلَّى اللهُ عَلَيْهِ وَسَلَّمَ أَوْصِنِيْ، قَالَ: لَاتَغْضَبْ. فَرَدَّدَ
مِرَارًا؛ قَالَ: لَاتَغْضَبْ - رَوَاهُ الْبُخَارِيُّ.

Translation:

Abū Hurayrah (*radiyallāhu 'anhu*) reported that a man said to the Prophet (*sallallāhu 'alayhi wasallam*), "Admonish me!" He said, "Do not get angry." (The man) repeated the request several times, but the Prophet answered, "Do not get angry."[1]

[Al-Bukhārī relates this.]

Note:

1. In another Ḥadīth, the Prophet *sallallāhu 'alayhi wasallam* said, "The powerful wrestler is not he who could knock down another, but really the one who could keep himself under control in anger". 'Alī (r.a.), in one of the battles, had knocked down a pagan challenger in a single duel and was about to kill him when the fallen enemy abused him and, according to some other version spat on him. 'Alī (r.a.), to the utter surprise of the pagan, restrained his hand and let him off. The baffled enemy questioned 'Alī (r.a.), who said, "I could kill you for the sake of Allah, but not for personal affront." This quality distinguishes a true Muslim (*Mu'min*) from the less cultured people. The *Mu'mins* are *those who shun the great sins and indecencies, and when they are angry even then forgive* (Qur'an, 42:37).

The Prophet *sallallāhu 'alayhi wasallam* advised believers to seek protection of Allah in their anger which is incited by Satan. He advised that when you are gripped by anger, then you should try to cool down by performing the ablutions. The washing of face, hands and feet would bring down the feverish heat of rage, and the time taken in this process would interpose delay between anger and rash action. He also recommended that in fits of anger, it would be better for a person to sit down if he was standing, and to lie down if he was already sitting. Modern research has proved that repeated over-stimulation of emotion in anger, is a potent cause of hypertension. It is significant to note that mastery of anger and exercise of restraint are inculcated as moral and social disciplines.

عَنْ أَبِيْ يَعْلَى شَدَّادِ بْنِ أَوْسٍ رَضِيَ اللهُ عَنْهُ عَنْ
رَسُوْلِ اللهِ صَلَّى اللهُ عَلَيْهِ وَسَلَّمَ قَالَ: إِنَّ اللهَ كَتَبَ
الْإِحْسَانَ عَلَى كُلِّ شَيْءٍ، فَإِذَا قَتَلْتُمْ فَأَحْسِنُوْا الْقِتْلَةَ،
وَإِذَا ذَبَحْتُمْ فَأَحْسِنُوْا الذِّبْحَةَ، وَلْيُحِدَّ أَحَدُكُمْ شَفْرَتَهُ
وَلْيُرِحْ ذَبِيْحَتَهُ - رَوَاهُ مُسْلِمٌ.

Translation:

Abū Ya'lā Shaddād bin Aus (*radiyallāhu 'anhu*) reported
that the Messenger of Allah (*sallallāhu 'alayhi wasallam*)
said, "Truly Allah has enjoined goodness (*ihsān*) with regard
to everything. So when you kill, kill in a good way; when
you slaughter, slaughter in a good way; so everyone of you
should sharpen his knife, and let the slaughtered animal die
comfortably."
[Muslim relates it.]

34

عَنْ أَبِيْ ذَرٍّ جُنْدُبِ بْنِ جُنَادَةَ وَأَبِيْ عَبْدِ الرَّحْمٰنِ مُعَاذِ
بْنِ جَبَلٍ رَضِيَ اللهُ عَنْهُمَا عَنْ رَسُوْلِ اللهِ صَلَّى اللهُ عَلَيْهِ
وَسَلَّمَ قَالَ: اِتَّقِ اللهَ حَيْثُمَا كُنْتَ وَأَتْبِعِ السَّيِّئَةَ الْحَسَنَةَ
تَمْحُهَا وَخَالِقِ النَّاسَ بِخُلُقٍ حَسَنٍ. رَوَاهُ التِّرْمِـذِيُّ،
وَقَـالَ: حَـدِيْثٌ حَسَنٌ. وَفِيْ بَعْضِ النُّسَـخِ حَسَنٌ
صَحِيْحٌ.

Translation:

Abū Dharr Jundub bin Junādah al-Ghifāri and Abū 'Abd al-Rahmān Mu'ādh bin Jabal (*radiyallahu anhumā*) reported that the Messenger of Allah (*sallallāhu 'alayhi wasallam*) said, "Fear Allah wheresoever you may be; follow up an evil deed by a good one which will wipe (the former) out, and behave good-naturedly to people."

[Al-Tirmidhī relates it, saying: It is a good (*hasan*) Tradition. In some copies he says: It is a good and genuine (*hasan* and *sahīh*) Hadīth.]

عَنْ أَبِي الْعَبَّاسِ عَبْدِ اللهِ بْنِ عَبَّاسٍ رَضِيَ اللهُ عَنْهُمَا

قَالَ : كُنْتُ خَلْفَ النَّبِيِّ صَلَّى اللهُ عَلَيْهِ وَسَلَّمَ يَوْمًا فَقَالَ :

يَاغُلَامُ إِنِّي أُعَلِّمُكَ كَلِمَاتٍ : احْفَظِ اللهَ يَحْفَظْكَ ، احْفَظِ

اللهَ تَجِدْهُ تُجَاهَكَ ، إِذَا سَأَلْتَ فَاسْأَلِ اللهَ ، وَإِذَا اسْتَعَنْتَ

فَاسْتَعِنْ بِاللهِ . وَاعْلَمْ أَنَّ الْأُمَّةَ لَوِ اجْتَمَعَتْ عَلَى أَنْ

يَنْفَعُوكَ بِشَيْءٍ ، لَمْ يَنْفَعُوكَ إِلَّا بِشَيْءٍ قَدْ كَتَبَهُ اللهُ لَكَ ؛ وَإِنِ

اجْتَمَعُوا عَلَى أَنْ يَضُرُّوكَ بِشَيْءٍ ، لَمْ يَضُرُّوكَ إِلَّا بِشَيْءٍ قَدْ

كَتَبَهُ اللهُ عَلَيْكَ ، رُفِعَتِ الْأَقْلَامُ وَجَفَّتِ الصُّحُفُ . رَوَاهُ

التِّرْمِذِيُّ . وَقَالَ : حَدِيْثٌ حَسَنٌ صَحِيْحٌ .

وَفِيْ رِوَايَةٍ غَيْرِ التِّرْمِذِيِّ : احْفَظِ اللهَ تَجِدْهُ أَمَامَكَ

تَعَرَّفْ إِلَى اللهِ فِي الرَّخَاءِ يَعْرِفْكَ فِي الشِّدَّةِ ، وَاعْلَمْ أَنَّ

مَاأَخْطَأَكَ لَمْ يَكُنْ لِيُصِيْبَكَ وَمَاأَصَابَكَ لَمْ يَكُنْ لِيُخْطِئَكَ .

وَاعْلَمْ أَنَّ النَّصْرَ مَعَ الصَّبْرِ وَأَنَّ الْفَرَجَ مَعَ الْكَرْبِ وَأَنَّ

مَعَ الْعُسْرِ يُسْرًا .

Abū al-'Abbās 'Abdullāh bin 'Abbās (*radiyallāhu 'anhumā*) reported: I was behind the Prophet (*sallallāhu 'alayhi wasallam*) when he said, "O young man, I will teach you some words (of wisdom). Keep Allah in mind, He will preserve you. Keep Allah in mind, you will find Him in front of you. If you (have need to) ask, ask of Allah. And if you must seek help, seek help from Allah.[1] Know that even if the (whole) community is united to (do something to) benefit you in any matter, they would not benefit you in aught save what Allah has written for you, and even if they were united to harm you in any matter they would not harm you in aught save what Allah has already written for you. The pens had been lifted and the pages were dry."

[Al-Tirmidhī relates this and says: It is a good, genuine Hadīth.]

According to a line of transmission other than that of al-Tirmidhī (it reads):

"Keep Allah in mind and you will find Him in front of you. Get acquainted with Allah in days of ease and He will know you in days of distress. Know that what missed you could not have hit you, and what hit you could not have missed you. Know that victory comes with patience, relief follows distress, ease follows hardship."[2]

Notes:

1.   A Muslim repeats the Sūrah al-Fātihah at least 17 times a day in his daily prayers. Verse 4 of the Sūrah reads: *Thee alone we worship; and unto Thee alone we turn for aid.*

2.   *So, verily, with every difficulty, there is relief: verily with every difficulty there is relief. Therefore, when thou art free still labour hard. And to thy Lord turn (all) they attention* (Qur'an, 94:5-8).

عَنْ أَبِيْ مَسْعُوْدٍ عُقْبَةَ بْنِ عَمْـرِو الْأَنْصَـارِيِّ
الْبَدْرِيِّ رَضِيَ اللهُ عَنْهُ قَالَ : قَالَ رَسُوْلُ اللهِ صَلَّى اللهُ عَلَيْهِ
وَسَلَّمَ : إِنَّ مِمَّا أَدْرَكَ النَّاسُ مِنْ كَلَامِ النُّبُوَّةِ الْأُوْلَى إِذَا لَمْ
تَسْتَحِ فَاصْنَعْ مَاشِئْتَ – رَوَاهُ الْبُخَارِيُّ.

Translation:

Abū Mas'ūd 'Uqbah bin 'Amr al-Ansārī al-Badrī,*
(*radiyallāhu 'anhu*) reported that the Messenger of Allah
(*sallallāhu 'alayhi wasallam*) said, "Among the things that
people have found from the words of the earlier prophecy
was: 'If you have no shame, do whatever you wish.'"
[Al-Bukhārī relates it.]

* *al-Badrī* means one who was one of those who fought at Badr.

عَنْ أَبِيْ عَمْرٍو وَقِيْلَ أَبِيْ عَمْرَةَ سُفْيَانَ بْنِ عَبْدِ اللهِ
رَضِيَ اللهُ عَنْهُ قَالَ، قُلْتُ يَارَسُوْلَ اللهِ : قُـلْ لِيْ فِيْ
الْإِسْلَامِ قَوْلاً لَاأَسْأَلُ عَنْهُ أَحَدًا غَيْرَكَ، قَالَ : قُلْ آمَنْتُ
بِاللهِ ثُمَّ اسْتَقِمْ - رَوَاهُ مُسْلِمٌ .

Translation:

On the authority of Abū 'Amr, though others call (him) Abū
'Amrah Sufyān bin 'Abdullāh (*radiyallāhu 'anhu*) who said:
I said, "O Messenger of Allah, tell me something about
Islam which I could not ask anyone about save you". He
answered, "Say: 'I believe in Allah,' and then be steadfast
(in accordance with such a profession)."
[Muslim relates this.]

39

عَنْ أَبِيْ عَبْدِ اللهِ جَابِرِ بْنِ عَبْدِ اللهِ الْأَنْصَارِيِّ رَضِيَ
اللهُ عَنْهُمَا أَنَّ رَجُلًا سَأَلَ رَسُوْلَ اللهِ صَلَّى اللهُ عَلَيْهِ وَسَلَّمَ
فَقَالَ : أَرَأَيْتَ إِذَا صَلَّيْتُ الْمَكْتُوْبَاتِ وَصُمْتُ رَمَضَانَ
وَأَحْلَلْتُ الْحَلَالَ وَحَرَّمْتُ الْحَرَامَ وَلَمْ أَزِدْ عَلَى ذٰلِكَ شَيْئًا
أَدْخُلُ الْجَنَّةَ قَالَ : نَعَمْ. رَوَاهُ مُسْلِمٌ. وَمَعْنَى حَرَّمْتُ
الْحَرَامَ : اجْتَنَبْتُهُ. وَمَعْنَى أَحْلَلْتُ الْحَلَالَ : فَعَلْتُهُ مُعْتَقِدًا
حِلَّهُ.

Translation:

Abū 'Abdullāh Jābir bin 'Abdullāh al-Anṣārī (*radiyallāhu anhumā*) reported that a man questioned the Messenger of Allah (*sallallāhu 'alayhi wasallam*) saying, "Do you see, if I pray the prescribed (prayers), fast during Ramaḍān, allow myself what is lawful and forbid what is forbidden,[1] but do nothing more than that, shall I enter the Garden?" He (the Prophet (*sallallāhu 'alayhi wasallam*) answered: "Yes." [Muslim relates this.]

Note:

1. The meaning of "forbid what is forbidden" is "to avoid", and the meaning of "allow myself what is lawful" is "do it in the belief that it is allowed."

In another Ḥadīth, narrated by both al-Bukhārī and Muslim, Abū Hurayrah reported that an Arab came to the Prophet *sallallāhu 'alayhi wasallam* and said, "Guide me to an action which, if I do, will cetainly take me to Paradise." He said, "You shall serve Allah, shall not associate with Him anything, keep up the prescribed prayers, pay the obligatory *zakāt*, and keep fast of Ramadān." He replied, "By Him in whose hand my soul is, I shall not add anything to this or fall short of it." Then when he turned away the Prophet *sallallāhu 'alayhi wasallam* said, "If anyone wishes to look at a man who will be among the people of Paradise, let him look at this man" (*Mishkāt al-Masābih, bāb Imān*).

عَنْ أَبِيْ مَالِكٍ الْحَارِثِ بْنِ عَاصِمٍ الْأَشْعَرِيِّ رَضِيَ
اللهُ عَنْهُ قَالَ، قَالَ رَسُوْلُ اللهِ صَلَّى اللهُ وَسَلَّمَ: اَلطُّهُوْرُ
شَطْرُ الْإِيْمَانِ وَالْحَمْدُ للهِ تَمْلَأُ الْمِيْزَانَ، وَسُبْحَانَ اللهِ
وَالْحَمْدُ للهِ تَمْلَآنِ أَوْ تَمْلَأُ مَابَيْنَ السَّمَاءِ وَالْأَرْضِ،
وَالصَّلَاةُ نُوْرٌ وَالصَّدَقَةُ بُرْهَانٌ وَالصَّبْرُ ضِيَاءٌ، وَالْقُرْآنُ
حُجَّةٌ لَكَ أَوْ عَلَيْكَ، كُلُّ النَّاسِ يَغْدُوْ فَبَائِعٌ نَفْسَهُ،
فَمُعْتِقُهَا أَوْ مُوْبِقُهَا. رَوَاهُ مُسْلِمٌ.

Translation:

On the authority of Abū Mālik al-Hārith bin 'Āsim al-
Ash'arī (*radiyallāhu 'anhu*) who said: The Messenger of
Allah (*sallallāhu 'alayhi wasallam*) said, "Being purified[1]
(clean) is half of faith; saying '*Alhamdulillāh*' (Praise be to
God) fills the scales; and saying '*Subhānallāhi wa'l-
hamdulillāhi*' (Exalted be God and Praise be to God),[2] fill
or fill the space between the heavens and the earth; *salāt*
(prayers) is a light;[3] *Sadaqah* is a proof (of sincere faith);[4]
patience (*Sabr*) is a shining glory,[5] the Qur'an is a plea (an
argument) for you or against you.[6] All men rise at morn and
sell themselves, thereby setting themselves free or destroying
themselves."[7]
[Muslim relates it.]

1.   Personal cleanliness is index of the clean and neat habits of an individual. Outward cleanliness is the first step towards the purity of the soul. Very often both go together. So in Islam the personal cleanliness is part of faith, and cleanliness of the body from all types of filth and dirtines is compulsory before one enters prayer.   Ablutions are prescribed as an essential condition of prayer before Allah Who is the Essence of Purity. He likes His worshippers who are pure.

    Personal cleanliness is bound to be reflected in the social life of the people, in their cleanliness and sanitation of their houses and towns. In golden days of Islamic history, Muslims set up water supply system in Baghdad and Cordova, laid out gardens in their cities from Lahore to Samarkand and atttained a very high level of cleanliness, sanitation, and hygienic living.   But   today the Muslims have lost sight of this aspect of their Faith, and it is a shame to visit most of the Muslim villages and towns from one end of the Muslim world to the other end, from Morocco to Indonesia. The offensive dirt and putrid filth witnessed in most of the Muslim habitations now, is the very negation of the teachings of the Prophet, who was the first among Prophets to take the lead in social legislation and public hygiene. He was the embodiment of spotless cleanliness in his personal life.

2.   *Alhamdulillāh* means "all Praise is due to Allah" and *Subhānallāh* means "Glory to Allah". The repetition of these phrases relating to praise and glory of Allah brings innumerable spiritual benefits.

3.   "Prayer (*salāt*) is light" because by repetition of which the soul assumes light and brightness just as constant polish of things makes it bright after removing the rusts and other impurities that might have fallen upon it. It will be a light in the darkness of grave and on the Resurrection Day, and it removes darkness of mind and soul.

4.   Man will be asked about his surplus wealth on the

Resurrection Day. In that crisis, charity will stand up as a proof of his Faith to relieve him of his difficulties.

5.   Patience is said to be *diyā'*. *Diyā'* is an attribute of the Sun while *nūr* (light) of the moon. Sunshine is more perfect than the light of the moon. Patience is called shining and not light as it produces perfect light in mind. Patience in trials and calamities creates brightness just as the brightness of gold is seen after it is burnt by fire.

6.   "The Qur'an is plea or argument for or against you" means that if actions are done in accordance with the teachings of the Qur'an, it will plead for him on the Resurrection Day but on the other hand if his actions are not in accordance with the teachings of the Qur'an, it will plead against him.

7.   There are two courses left open to the soul - either to go to salvation or to destruction. If it sells itself to the pleasure of Allah, it will realise its true nature and if it sells itself to the pleasures of the world, it will bring its ruin. In other words, if it resigns itself entirely to the will of Allah and does deeds with that object of attaining the pleasure of Allah in view, it will attain its object and if on the other hand it is led by passion and all its activities are directed towards worldly motives, its efforts will be brought to nought.

عَنْ أَبِيْ ذَرٍّ الْغِفَارِيِّ رَضِيَ اللهُ عَنْهُ عَنِ النَّبِيِّ صَلَّى اللهُ عَلَيْهِ وَسَلَّمَ فِيْمَا يَرْوِيْهِ عَنْ رَبِّهِ عَزَّ وَجَلَّ أَنَّهُ قَالَ: يَاعِبَادِيْ إِنِّيْ حَرَّمْتُ الظُّلْمَ عَلَى نَفْسِيْ وَجَعَلْتُهُ بَيْنَكُمْ مُحَرَّمًا فَلَا تَظَالَمُوْا. يَاعِبَادِيْ كُلُّكُمْ ضَالٌّ إِلَّا مَنْ هَدَيْتُهُ فَاسْتَهْدُوْنِيْ أَهْدِكُمْ. يَاعِبَادِيْ كُلُّكُمْ جَائِعٌ إِلَّا مَنْ أَطْعَمْتُهُ فَاسْتَطْعِمُوْنِيْ أُطْعِمْكُمْ. يَاعِبَادِيْ كُلُّكُمْ عَارٍ إِلَّا مَنْ كَسَوْتُهُ فَاسْتَكْسُوْنِيْ أَكْسُكُمْ. يَاعِبَادِيْ إِنَّكُمْ تُخْطِئُوْنَ بِاللَّيْلِ وَالنَّهَارِ وَأَنَا أَغْفِرُ الذُّنُوْبَ جَمِيْعًا فَاسْتَغْفِرُوْنِيْ أَغْفِرْ لَكُمْ. يَاعِبَادِيْ إِنَّكُمْ لَنْ تَبْلُغُوْا ضُرِّيْ فَتَضُرُّوْنِيْ وَلَنْ تَبْلُغُوْا نَفْعِيْ فَتَنْفَعُوْنِيْ. يَاعِبَادِيْ لَوْ أَنَّ أَوَّلَكُمْ وَآخِرَكُمْ وَإِنْسَكُمْ وَجِنَّكُمْ كَانُوْا عَلَى أَتْقَى قَلْبِ رَجُلٍ وَاحِدٍ مِنْكُمْ مَازَادَ ذَلِكَ فِيْ مُلْكِيْ شَيْئًا. يَاعِبَادِيْ لَوْ أَنَّ أَوَّلَكُمْ وَآخِرَكُمْ وَإِنْسَكُمْ وَجِنَّكُمْ كَانُوْا عَلَى أَفْجَرِ قَلْبِ رَجُلٍ وَاحِدٍ مِنْكُمْ مَانَقَصَ ذَلِكَ مِنْ مُلْكِيْ شَيْئًا. يَاعِبَادِيْ لَوْ أَنَّ أَوَّلَكُمْ وَآخِرَكُمْ وَإِنْسَكُمْ وَجِنَّكُمْ قَامُوْا فِيْ صَعِيْدٍ وَاحِدٍ فَسَأَلُوْنِيْ فَأَعْطَيْتُ كُلَّ وَاحِدٍ مَسْأَلَتَهُ مَانَقَصَ

45

ذٰلِكَ مِمَّا عِنْدِيْ إِلاَّ كَمَا يَنْقُصُ الْمِخْيَطُ إِذَا أُدْخِلَ الْبَحْرَ .

يَاعِبَادِيْ إِنَّمَا هِيَ أَعْمَالُكُمْ أُحْصِيْهَا لَكُمْ ثُمَّ أُوَفِّيْكُمْ إِيَّاهَا

فَمَنْ وَجَدَ خَيْرًا فَلْيَحْمَدِ اللهَ وَمَنْ وَجَدَ غَيْرَ ذٰلِكَ فَلاَ

يَلُوْمَنَّ إِلاَّ نَفْسَهُ - رَوَاهُ مُسْلِمٌ .

Translation:

It was related on the authority of Abū Dharr al-Ghifārī
(*radiyallāhu 'anhu*) that the Prophet (*sallallāhu 'alayhi
wasallam*) said, of what he related from his Lord, magnified
and exalted be He, Who said: "O My servants, I have made
oppression unlawful for Me and unlawful for you, so do not
commit oppression against one another. My servants, all of
you are liable to err except one whom I guide on the right
path, so seek right guidance from Me so that I should direct
you to the right path. O My servants, all of you are hungry
(needy) except one whom I feed, so beg food from Me, so
that I may give that to you. O My servants, all of you are
naked (need clothes) except one whom I provide garments,
so beg clothes from Me, so that I should clothe you. O My
servants, you commit error night and day and I am there to
pardon your sins, so beg pardon from Me so that I should
grant you pardon. O My servants, you can neither do Me
any harm nor can you do Me any good. O My servants,
even if the first amongst you and the last amongst you and
even the whole of human race of yours, and that of Jinns
even, become (equal in) God-conscious like the heart of a
single person amongst you, nothing would add to My Power.
O My servants, even if the first amongst you and the last
amongst you and the whole of the human race of yours and
that of Jinns too in unison become the most wicked (all
beating) like the heart of a single person, it would cause no
loss to My Power. O My servants, even if the first amongst

46

you and the last amongst you and the whole human race of yours and that of Jinns also all stand in one plain ground and you ask Me and I confer upon every person what he asks for, it would not, in any way, cause any loss to Me (even less) than that which is caused to the ocean by dipping the needle in it. My servants, these deeds of your which I am recording for you I shall reward you for them, so he who finds good should praise Allah and he who does not find that should not blame anyone but his ownself.
[Muslim related this.]

Notes:

1. The verb *zalama*, from which the noun *zulm* is derived, generally means 'he did wrong' or 'acted wrongfully', injuriously, or tyrannically. These translations are incorrect in their own way, but in the Qur'an, the word *al-zulm* signifies the putting of a thing in a place not its own, or putting it in a wrong place, or misplacing it; it may also mean transgressing the proper limit much or little.

Thus in the light of these meanings of the word *zulm*, as used in this Hadīth, implies that Allah does no wrong; whatever He does is based on justice; even when He punishes His servants He does what is good for them.

So far as oppression on the part of human beings is concerned, it means high-handedness upon one another. (*Sahīh Muslim*, English translation by Abdul Hamid Siddiqui, p.1365)

47

عَنْ أَبِيْ ذَرٍّ رَضِيَ اللهُ عَنْهُ أَيْضًا أَنَّ أُنَاسًا مِنْ
أَصْحَابِ رَسُوْلِ اللهِ صَلَّى اللهُ عَلَيْهِ وَسَلَّمَ قَالُوْا لِلنَّبِيِّ
صَلَّى اللهُ عَلَيْهِ وَسَلَّمَ: يَارَسُوْلَ اللهِ: ذَهَبَ أَهْلُ الدُّثُوْرِ
بِالْأُجُوْرِ يُصَلُّوْنَ كَمَا نُصَلِّيْ وَيَصُوْمُوْنَ كَمَا نَصُوْمُ
وَيَتَصَدَّقُوْنَ بِفُضُوْلِ أَمْوَالِهِمْ. قَالَ: أَوَلَيْسَ قَدْ جَعَلَ اللهُ
لَكُمْ مَاتَصَدَّقُوْنَ إِنَّ بِكُلِّ تَسْبِيْحَةٍ صَدَقَةً وَكُلِّ تَكْبِيْرَةٍ
صَدَقَةً وَكُلِّ تَحْمِيْدَةٍ صَدَقَةً وَكُلِّ تَهْلِيْلَةٍ صَدَقَةً وَأَمْرٍ
بِالْمَعْرُوْفِ صَدَقَةً وَنَهْيٍ عَنْ مُنْكَرٍ صَدَقَةً وَفِيْ بُضْعِ
أَحَدِكُمْ صَدَقَةً. قَالُوْا يَارَسُوْلَ اللهِ: أَيَأْتِيْ أَحَدُنَا شَهْوَتَهُ
وَيَكُوْنُ لَهُ فِيْهَا أَجْرٌ، قَالَ: أَرَأَيْتُمْ لَوْ وَضَعَهَا فِيْ حَرَامٍ
أَكَانَ عَلَيْهِ وِزْرٌ فَكَذَلِكَ إِذَا وَضَعَهَا فِيْ الْحَلَالِ كَانَ لَهُ
أَجْرٌ- رَوَاهُ مُسْلِمٌ.

Translation:

Abū Dharr (*radiyallāhu 'anhu*) reported that some of the
people from among the companions of the Apostle of Allah
(*sallallāhu 'alayhi wasallam*) said to him, "Messenger of

Allah, the rich have taken away (all the) reward. They observe prayer as we do, they keep the fasts as we keep them, and they give *sadaqah* from their surplus riches." Upon this he (the Holy Prophet) said: "Has Allah not prescribed for you (a course) by following which you can (also) do *sadaqah*? In every *tasbīh* (declaration of the glorification of Allah i.e. saying *Subhānallāh*) there is a *sadaqah*, every *takbīr* (i.e. saying *Allāhu Akbar*) is a *sadaqah*, every *tahmīd* (praise of Him saying *Alhamdulillāh*) is a *sadaqah*, every *tahlīl* (saying *Lā ilāha illallāh*, there is no god but Allah) is a *sadaqah*,[1] enjoining of good is a *sadaqah*, forbidding of that which is evil is a *sadaqah*, and in man's sexual intercourse (with his wife) there is a *sadaqah*." They (the companions) said, "Messenger of Allah, is there reward for him who satisfies his sexual passion among us?" He said: "Tell me, if he were to devote it to something forbidden, would it not be a sin on his part? Similarly, if he were to devote it to something lawful, he should have a reward."
[Muslim relates this.]

Note:

1. It should be remembered that the *tasbīh, tahmīd, takbīr* etc. are not a substitute for *sadaqah* but an alternative for the poor to earn the same reward the rich may earn by giving *sadaqah*. The rich on the other hand should not think that by resorting to *tasbīh, tahmīd* etc. alone, they could escape the punishment of Allah if they hoard their wealth and do not show their gratitude to Allah for their wealth by spending *of that whereof He hath made you trustees* (Qur'an, 24:33). Their *'ibādah* will not be accepted unless accompanied by *sadaqah*.

In the Qur'an *zakāt* is mentioned side by side with *salāt* on as many as 82 occasions. The command: *Be steadfast in prayer; practise regular charity* actually runs through it. Apart from it, where the distinguishing qualities of Muslims are set forth in the

Qur'an, it is invariably pointed out that *They establish Prayer and practise regular charity*. It is related by 'Abdullāh bin 'Umar that the Prophet once said to him, "I have been commanded to wage war against the people until they testify that there is no one worthy of worship save Allah and Muhammad is His Apostle, and establish *salāt*, and pay the *zakāt*. If they do so, they obtain the security of life and property from me except for the rights of Islam, and their account is with God." (*See Hadīth 8 in this volume*).

In real life we see rich Muslims who are outwardly pious with their devotions but when it comes to *zakāt* they avoid the issue with various excuses. They are no different from the rebels who refused to pay *zakāt* against whom Abū Bakr (r.a.) waged war and put down with a heavy hand. Abū Bakr (r.a.) was explicit: "I will certainly wage war against those who make a distinction between *salāt* and *zakāt* for *zakāt* is the rightful claim of the goods. I swear that if they refuse to give even a kid which they used to give during the days of the Prophet I will make war on them".

Sadaqah is a visible expression of man's love for God. It signifies that he is prepared to sacrifice every cherished thing or desire for the sake of Allah. Thus it is a symbol of man's devotion to God. As it is an expression of devoted and pious heart, it can, therefore, manifest itself in every act of piety. Remembrance of Allah, performing religious duties with full sense of responsibility, doing of good acts and asking others to do them, refraining from evil and persuading others to shun them, observing of the limits imposed by the Lord on what is lawful and unlawful - all these acts are the acts of *sadaqah*. In fact the whole life spent in devotion to Allah is a *sadaqah* for it shows the love of God. The Holy Prophet *sallallāhu 'alayhi wasallam* had made it clear that sex is not evil in itself. It has, however, imposed limits upon its use, so that it may not become the misuse of something which is basically pure. Thus the limits set upon sex do not aim at taking the joy out of life, but to provide us the signposts "in order to protect our happiness and to help make our life's journey as 'tragedy free' as possible" (*Sahīh Muslim,* English translation by A.H. Siddiqui, p.482).

50

عَنْ أَبِيْ هُرَيْرَةَ رَضِيَ اللهُ عَنْهُ قَالَ، قَالَ رَسُوْلُ اللهِ
صَلَّى اللهُ عَلَيْهِ وَسَلَّمَ: كُـلُّ سُلَامَى مِنَ النَّاسِ عَلَيْهِ
صَدَقَةٌ كُلَّ يَوْمٍ تَطْلُعُ فِيْهِ الشَّمْسُ تَعْدِلُ بَيْنَ اثْنَيْنِ صَدَقَةٌ
وَتُعِيْنُ الرَّجُلَ فِيْ دَابَّتِهِ فَتَحْمِلُهُ عَلَيْهَا أَوْ تَرْفَعُ لَهُ عَلَيْهَا
مَتَاعَهُ صَدَقَةٌ وَالْكَلِمَةُ الطَّيِّبَةُ صَدَقَةٌ وَبِكُلِّ خَطْوَةٍ تَمْشِيْهَا
إِلَى الصَّلَاةِ صَدَقَةٌ وَتُمِيْطُ الْأَذَى عَنِ الطَّرِيْقِ صَدَقَةٌ .
رَوَاهُ الْبُخَارِيُّ وَمُسْلِمٌ .

Translation:

Abū Hurayrah (*radiyallāhu 'anhu*) reported that the
Messenger of Allah (*sallallāhu 'alayhi wasallam*) said, "On
every bone of men's fingers and toes, there is *sadaqah* every
day the sun rises. Doing justice between two men is
sadaqah, and assisting a man (to ride) upon his animal that
it may carry him, or lifting up his luggage upon it is
sadaqah, and a good word is *sadaqah* and every step he
takes towards prayer (*salat*) is *sadaqah*, and removing
harmful things from pathway is *sadaqah*."[1]
[Al-Bukhārī and Muslim both relate this.]

Note:

1.   The subject matter of this Hadīth is the same as that of the
last one. *Sadaqah* has an unlimited scope in Islam, and the word
'charity' in English does not convey the full meaning and import

of the word *sadaqah*. *Sadaqah* not only means that giving of charity in money or goods to the poor and deserving but also includes many charitable acts, big and small, which are either ignored or considered too trivial. The exercise of charity can range from the highest actions like the administration of justice, teaching, and ministering to the sick, to the smallest but significant actions like helping a blind to cross the road, and protecting the children from the rush traffic. Surely the list of charity has been enlarged in our modern times by the changes in our way of living. Queuing up for one's turn in public places, for example, may be considered as an act of charity. In the olden days the stones and thorns were found on the paths, but now different types of obstacles and hazards threaten life on the roads and waterways, and anybody who minimises or removes these dangers, performs an act of charity. The people of the developing nations have a lot to gain from this general and all-embracing concept of charity. Children should be taught not to litter in gardens and public places, and should be told that it is an act of charity to help keep our environment clean.

عَنِ النَّوَّاسِ بْنِ سِمْعَانَ رَضِيَ اللهُ عَنْهُ عَنِ النَّبِيِّ صَلَّى اللهُ عَلَيْهِ وَسَلَّمَ قَالَ: اَلْبِرُّ حُسْنُ الْخُلُقِ وَالْإِثْمُ مَاحَاكَ فِيْ نَفْسِكَ وَكَرِهْتَ أَنْ يَطَّلِعَ عَلَيْهِ النَّاسُ - رَوَاهُ مُسْلِمٌ.

وَعَنْ وَابِصَةَ بْنِ مَعْبَدٍ رَضِيَ اللهُ عَنْهُ قَالَ: أَتَيْتُ رَسُوْلَ اللهِ صَلَّى اللهُ عَلَيْهِ وَسَلَّمَ فَقَالَ: جِئْتَ تَسْأَلُ عَنِ الْبِرِّ؟ قُلْتُ: نَعَمْ! قَالَ: اسْتَفْتِ قَلْبَكَ، اَلْبِرُّ مَااطْمَأَنَّتْ إِلَيْهِ النَّفْسُ وَاطْمَأَنَّ إِلَيْهِ الْقَلْبُ وَالْإِثْمُ مَاحَاكَ فِي النَّفْسِ وَتَرَدَّدَ فِي الصَّدْرِ، وَإِنْ أَفْتَاكَ النَّاسُ وَأَفْتَوْكَ. حَدِيْثٌ حَسَنٌ؛ رَوَيْنَاهُ فِيْ مُسْنَدَيِ الْإِمَامَيْنِ أَحْمَدَ بْنِ حَنْبَلٍ وَالدَّارِمِيِّ بِإِسْنَادٍ حَسَنٍ.

Translation:

Al-Nawwās bin Sam'ān (*raḍiyallāhu 'anhu*) reported that the Prophet (*sallallāhu 'alayhi wasallam*) said, "Righteousness is good character, and sin is that which rankles in your heart about which you do not want people to know."
[Muslim related this.]

According to Wābiṣah bin Ma'bad (*raḍiyallāhu 'anhu*) who

53

said: I came to the Messenger of Allah (*sallallāhu 'alayhi wasallam*) who said, "You have come to ask about righteousness?" "Yes," I answered. He said, "Ask your own heart for a *fatwa*. Righteousness is when the soul feels peace and the heart feels peace, and sin is what creates restlessness in the soul, and rumbles in the bosom, even though people give their opinion (in your favour) and continue to do so."

[An excellent Hadīth which we have narrated according to the two *Musnads*, that of Ahmad bin Hanbal and that of al-Dārimī, with excellent *isnāds*.]

عَنْ أَبِيْ نَجِيْحٍ اَلْعِرْبَاضِ بْنِ سَارِيَةَ رَضِيَ اللهُ عَنْهُ
قَالَ، وَعَظَنَا رَسُوْلُ اللهِ صَلَّى اللهُ عَلَيْهِ وَسَلَّمَ مَوْعِظَةً
وَجِلَتْ مِنْهَا الْقُلُوْبُ، وَذَرَفَتْ مِنْهَا الْعُيُوْنُ. فَقُلْنَا:
يَارَسُوْلَ اللهِ، كَأَنَّهَا مَوْعِـظَةُ مُوَدِّعٍ فَأَوْصِنَا. قَالَ:
أُوْصِيْكُمْ بِتَقْوَى اللهِ عَزَّ وَجَلَّ وَالسَّمْعِ وَالطَّاعَةِ وَإِنْ
تَأَمَّرَ عَلَيْكُمْ عَبْدٌ فَإِنَّهُ مَنْ يَعِشْ مِنْكُمْ فَسَيَرَى اخْتِلَافًا
كَثِيْرًا، فَعَلَيْكُمْ بِسُنَّتِيْ وَسُنَّةِ الْخُلَفَاءِ الرَّاشِدِيْنَ الْمَهْدِيِّيْنَ،
عَضُّوْا عَلَيْهَا بِالنَّوَاجِذِ. وَإِيَّاكُمْ وَمُحْدَثَاتِ اْلأُمُوْرِ فَإِنَّ كُلَّ
بِدْعَةٍ ضَلَالَةٌ - رَوَاهُ أَبُوْ دَاوُدَ وَالتِّرْمِذِيُّ، وَقَالَ: حَدِيْثٌ
حَسَنٌ صَحِيْحٌ.

Translation:

It was narrated on the authority of Abū Najīh al-'Irbād bin
Sāriyah (*radiyallāhu 'anhu*) who said: The Messenger of
Allah (*sallallāhu 'alayhi wasallam*) gave us a discourse
which filled our hearts with fear and made our eyes shed
tears, so we said, "O Messenger of Allah, it is as though this
were a farewell sermon, so give us an injunction." He then
said: "I enjoin you to fear Allah - magnified and exalted be
He! - and that you harken and obey, even should it be that
a slave is made a ruler over you. He among you who lives
long enough will see many differences, so for you is to

observe my *Sunnah* and the *Sunnah* of the rightly-guided Caliphs, holding on to them with your molar teeth. Beware of matters newly-introduced, for every innovation (*bid'ah*) is an error."

[Abū Dāwud relates it, as does al-Tirmidhī, who says: An excellent, genuine Ḥadīth.]

عَنْ مُعَاذِ بْنِ جَبَلٍ رَضِيَ اللهُ عَنْهُ قَالَ، قُلْتُ: يَارَسُوْلَ اللهِ أَخْبِرْنِيْ بِعَمَلٍ يُدْخِلُنِيْ الْجَنَّةَ وَيُبَاعِدُنِيْ عَنِ النَّارِ. قَالَ: لَقَدْ سَأَلْتَ عَنْ عَظِيْمٍ، وَإِنَّهُ لَيَسِيْرٌ عَلَى مَنْ يَسَّرَهُ اللهُ تَعَالَى عَلَيْهِ. تَعْبُدُ اللهَ لَاتُشْرِكُ بِهِ شَيْئًا، وَتُقِيْمُ الصَّلَاةَ، وَتُؤْتِيْ الزَّكَاةَ، وَتَصُوْمُ رَمَضَانَ، وَتَحُجُّ الْبَيْتَ. ثُمَّ قَالَ: أَلَا أَدُلُّكَ عَلَى أَبْوَابِ الْخَيْرِ؟ الصَّوْمُ جُنَّةٌ، وَالصَّدَقَةُ تُطْفِىءُ الْخَطِيْئَةَ كَمَا يُطْفِىءُ الْمَاءُ النَّارَ، وَصَلَاةُ الرَّجُلِ فِيْ جَوْفِ اللَّيْلِ. ثُمَّ تَلَا: تَتَجَافَى جُنُوْبُهُمْ عَنِ الْمَضَاجِعِ.... حَتَّى بَلَغَ... يَعْمَلُوْنَ. ثُمَّ قَالَ: أَلَا أُخْبِرُكَ بِرَأْسِ الْأَمْرِ وَعَمُوْدِهِ وَذِرْوَةِ سَنَامِهِ. قُلْتُ: بَلَى يَارَسُوْلَ اللهِ. قَالَ: رَأْسُ الْأَمْرِ الْإِسْلَامُ، وَعَمُوْدُهُ الصَّلَاةُ، وَذِرْوَةُ سَنَامِهِ الْجِهَادُ. ثُمَّ قَالَ: أَلَا أُخْبِرُكَ بِمِلَاكِ ذٰلِكَ كُلِّهِ. قُلْتُ: بَلَى يَارَسُوْلَ اللهِ. فَأَخَذَ بِلِسَانِهِ. وَقَالَ: كُفَّ عَلَيْكَ هٰذَا. قُلْتُ: يَانَبِيَّ اللهِ وَإِنَّا لَمُؤَاخَذُوْنَ بِمَانَتَكَلَّمُ بِهِ. فَقَالَ: ثَكِلَتْكَ أُمُّكَ، وَهَلْ يَكُبُّ النَّاسَ فِي النَّارِ عَلَى وُجُوْهِهِمْ. أَوْ قَالَ: عَلَى مَنَاخِرِهِمْ إِلاَّ حَصَائِدُ أَلْسِنَتِهِمْ - رَوَاهُ التِّرْمِذِيُّ. وَقَالَ: حَدِيْثٌ حَسَنٌ صَحِيْحٌ.

Translation:

From Mu'ādh bin Jabal (*radiyallāhu 'anhu*) who said: I said, "O Messenger of Allah, tell me of a deed which will bring me into the Garden and keep me away from the Fire." He said: "You have asked about a great matter, yet it is, indeed, an easy matter for him to whom Allah Most High makes it easy. (It is) that you worship Allah without associating anything with Him, that you perform the prayers (*salāt*), give the *zakāt*, fast during Ramadān, and go on pilgrimage to the House." Then he said, "Shall I not guide you to the gates of goodness? Fasting is a protection; *sadaqah* quenches wrong actions as water quenches fire; and a man's prayer in the middle of the night." Then he recited: *They forsake their beds* until he reached (the words) *they have been doing* [Qur'an, 32:16-17]. Then he said, "Shall I not also inform you about the head and the pillar (support) of the matter and the top of its hump?" I answered, "Surely! O Messenger of Allah." He then said, "The head of the matter is Islam and the pillar is the prayers, and the top of its hump is *jihād*." Then he said, "And shall I not inform you of the controlling of all that?" I answered, "Surely! O Messenger of Allah." So he took hold of his tongue and said, "Restrain this." I answered, "O Prophet of Allah, we indeed are blameworthy for all we speak with it." He said. "May your mother be bereft of you! Will anything but the harvests of their tongues overthrow men in hell on their faces (or he said, on their nostrils)?"

[Al-Tirmidhī relates it, saying: It is an excellent, sound Hadīth.]

عَنْ أَبِيْ ثَعْلَبَةَ الْخُشَنِيِّ جُرْثُوْمِ بْنِ نَاشِرٍ رَضِيَ اللهُ
عَنْهُ عَنْ رَسُوْلِ اللهِ صَلَّى اللهُ عَلَيْهِ وَسَلَّمَ قَالَ: إِنَّ اللهَ
تَعَالَى فَرَضَ فَرَائِضَ فَلَاتُضَيِّعُوْهَا، وَحَدَّ حُدُوْدًا
فَلَاتَعْتَدُوْهَا، وَحَرَّمَ أَشْيَاءَ فَلَاتَنْتَهِكُوْهَا، وَسَكَتَ عَنْ
أَشْيَاءَ رَحْمَةً لَكُمْ غَيْرَ نِسْيَانٍ فَلَاتَبْحَثُوْا عَنْهَا. حَدِيْثٌ
حَسَنٌ. رَوَاهُ الدَّارَقُطْنِيْ وَغَيْرُهُ.

Translation:

It was narrated on the authority of Abū Thaʿlabah al-
Khushanī Jurthūm bin Nāshir (*radiyallāhu 'anhu*) that the
Messenger of Allah (*sallallāhu 'alayhi wasallam*) said,
"Truly Allah the Most High has ordained certain duties, so
neglect them not; He has laid down certain limits, so do not
transgress them; He has forbidden certain things, do not
indulge in them; and He has said nothing about certain
things, as an act of mercy to you, not out of forgetfulness,
so do not go enquiring into these."[1]
[An excellent Tradition which al-Daraqutnī and others have related.]

Note:

1. *O ye who believe! Ask not questions about things which, if
made plain to you, may cause you trouble. But if ye ask about
things when the Qur'an is being revealed, they will be made plain
to you. Allah will forgive those: For Allah is Oft-Forgiving, Most
Forbearing. Some people before you did ask such questions, and
on that account lost their faith* (Qur'an 5:101-102, 'Abdullāh Yūsuf
'Alī's translation. *See also his note 807 on p.280*).

عَنْ أَبِي الْعَبَّاسِ سَهْلِ بْنِ سَعْدٍ السَّاعِدِيِّ رَضِيَ
اللهُ عَنْهُ قَالَ : جَاءَ رَجُلٌ إِلَى النَّبِيِّ صَلَّى اللهُ عَلَيْهِ وَسَلَّمَ ،
فَقَالَ : يَارَسُوْلَ اللهِ دُلَّنِيْ عَلَى عَمَلٍ إِذَا عَمِلْتُهُ أَحَبَّنِيْ اللهُ
وَأَحَبَّنِيْ النَّاسُ . فَقَالَ : اِزْهَدْ فِي الدُّنْيَا يُحِبَّكَ اللهُ وَازْهَدْ
فِيْمَا عِنْدَ النَّاسِ يُحِبَّكَ النَّاسُ . حَدِيْثٌ حَسَنٌ . رَوَاهُ ابْنُ
مَاجَهْ وَغَيْرُهُ بِأَسَانِيْدَ حَسَنَةٍ .

Translation:

From Abū al-'Abbās Sahl bin Sa'd al-Sā'idī (*radiyallāhu 'anhu*) who said: A man came to the Prophet (*sallallāhu 'alayhi wasallam*) saying, "O Messenger of Allah, show me a work which if I do it, will endear me to Allah and endear me to the people." He (*sallallāhu 'alayhi wasallam*) answered: "Be indifferent to the world and Allah will love you; be indifferent to what people have, and they will love you."

[An excellent Hadīth which Ibn Mājah and others relate, with an excellent *isnād*.]

اَلْحَدِيْثُ الثَّانِيْ وَالثَّلَاثُوْنَ

عَنْ أَبِيْ سَعِيْدٍ سَعْدِ بْنِ مَالِكِ بْنِ سِنَانٍ اَلْخُدْرِيّ
رَضِيَ اللهُ عَنْهُ أَنَّ رَسُوْلَ اللهِ صَلَّى اللهُ عَلَيْهِ وَسَلَّمَ قَالَ:
لَاضَرَرَ وَلَاضِرَارَ – حَدِيْثٌ حَسَنٌ. رَوَاهُ اِبْنُ مَاجَهْ
وَالدَّارُقُطْنِيُّ وَغَيْرُهُمَا مُسْنَدًا. وَرَوَاهُ مَالِكٌ فِيْ الْمُوَطَّإِ
مُرْسَلًا عَنْ عَمْرِو بْنِ يَحْيَى عَنْ أَبِيْهِ عَنِ النَّبِيِّ صَلَّى اللهُ
عَلَيْهِ وَسَلَّمَ فَأَسْقَطَ أَبَاسَعِيْدٍ وَلَهُ طُرُقٌ يُقَـوِّيْ بَعْضُهَا
بَعْضًا.

Translation:

It was related on the authority of Abū Saʿīd Saʿd bin Mālik bin Sinān al-Khudrī (*radiyallāhu ʿanhu*) that the Messenger (*sallallāhu ʿalayhi wasallam*) said, "No harm, no harming" (In other words, where there is no injury there is no requital).

[An excellent Hadīth which Ibn Mājah, al-Daraqutnī and others related as of sound *isnād*, but which Mālik related in his *Muwatta'*, as of broken *isnād*, from ʿAmr bin Yahyā, from his father, from the Prophet (*sallallāhu ʿalayhi wasallam*) but dropping (the name of) Abū Saʿīd. (This Hadīth) has lines of transmission which strengthen one another (so that it may be regarded as of sound *isnād*).]

عَنِ ابْنِ عَبَّاسٍ رَضِيَ اللهُ عَنْهُمَا أَنَّ رَسُوْلَ اللهِ صَلَّى اللهُ عَلَيْهِ وَسَلَّمَ قَالَ : لَوْ يُعْطَى النَّاسُ بِدَعْوَاهُمْ لَاَدَّعَى رِجَالٌ أَمْوَالَ قَوْمٍ وَدِمَاءَهُمْ لٰكِنِ الْبَيِّنَةُ عَلَى الْمُدَّعِيْ وَالْيَمِيْنُ عَلَى مَنْ أَنْكَرَ .

حَدِيْثٌ حَسَنٌ، رَوَاهُ الْبَيْهَقِيْ وَغَيْرُهُ هٰكَذَا وَبَعْضُهُ فِي الصَّحِيْحَيْنِ .

Translation:

Ibn 'Abbās (*radiyallāhu anhumā*) said that the Messenger of Allah (*sallallāhu 'alayhi wasallam*) said, "Were the people to be given what they claim, men would be laying claim to the property of a community and even to their blood. The onus of proof is on the one who makes the claim, and the oath is for him who denies."

[An excellent Ḥadīth, which al-Bayhaqī and others have related thus. Part of it is in the two Ṣaḥīḥ books (i.e. in al-Bukhārī and Muslim).]

عَنْ أَبِيْ سَعِيْدٍ الْخُدْرِيِّ رَضِيَ اللهُ عَنْهُ قَالَ : سَمِعْتُ رَسُوْلَ اللهِ صَلَّى اللهُ عَلَيْهِ وَسَلَّمَ يَقُوْلُ : مَنْ رَأَى مِنْكُمْ مُنْكَرًا فَلْيُغَيِّرْهُ بِيَدِهِ ، فَإِنْ لَمْ يَسْتَطِعْ فَبِلِسَانِهِ ، فَإِنْ لَمْ يَسْتَطِعْ فَبِقَلْبِهِ ، وَذٰلِكَ أَضْعَفُ الْإِيْمَانِ - رَوَاهُ مُسْلِمٌ .

Translation:

From Abū Sa'īd al-Khudrī (*radiyallāhu 'anhu*) who said: I heard the Messenger of Allah (*sallallāhu 'alayhi wasallam*) say, "When any one of you notices anything that is disapproved (of by Allah), let him change it with his hand, or if that is not possible, then with his tongue, or if that is not possible, then with his heart, though that is the weakest (kind of) faith."

[Muslim relates this.]

عَنْ أَبِيْ هُرَيْرَةَ رَضِيَ اللهُ عَنْهُ قَالَ، قَالَ رَسُوْلُ اللهِ
صَلَّى اللهُ عَلَيْهِ وَسَلَّمَ: لَاتَحَاسَدُوْا وَلَاتَنَاجَشُوْا
وَلَاتَبَاغَضُوْا وَلَاتَدَابَرُوْا وَلَا يَبِعْ بَعْضُكُمْ عَلَى بَيْعِ
بَعْضٍ وَكُوْنُوْا عِبَادَ اللهِ إِخْوَانًا، اَلْمُسْلِمُ أَخُو الْمُسْلِمِ
لَايَظْلِمُهُ وَلَايَخْذُلُهُ وَلَايَكْذِبُهُ وَلَايَحْقِرُهُ. التَّقْوَى هٰهُنَا،
وَيُشِيْرُ إِلَى صَدْرِهِ ثَلَاثَ مَرَّاتٍ. بِحَسْبِ امْرِىءٍ مِنَ الشَّرِّ
أَنْ يَحْقِرَ أَخَاهُ الْمُسْلِمَ، كُلُّ الْمُسْلِمِ عَلَى الْمُسْلِمِ حَرَامٌ دَمُهُ
وَمَالُهُ وَعِرْضُهُ - رَوَاهُ مُسْلِمٌ.

Translation:

Abū Hurayrah (*radiyallāhu 'anhu*) reported that the Messenger of Allah (*sallallāhu 'alayhi wasallam*) said, "Do not envy one another; do not outbid one another,[1] do not hate one another, do not shun one another and don't enter into a transaction when the others have entered into that transaction; and be as fellow-brothers and servants of Allah. A Muslim is the brother of a Muslim. He neither oppresses him nor humiliates him nor looks down upon him. The piety is here, (and while saying so) he pointed towards his chest thrice. It is a serious evil for a Muslim that he should look down upon his brother Muslim. All things of a Muslim are inviolable for his brother in faith; his blood, his wealth and his honour.

[Muslim relates this.]

Notes:

1.   *Lā tanājashū* means "do not practice *najash* or *najsh*".
Najasha signifies "he augmented the price of an article of
merchandise, not desiring to purchase it, but in order that another
might hear him and augment in the same manner, or he outbade in
a sale, in order that another might fall into a snare, he himself not
wanting the thing. It sometimes signifies the doing so in the case
of a dowry, in order that the doing so may be heard, and the
amount may consequently be augmented (Lane's *Arabic-English
Lexicon*, p.2771).

عَنْ أَبِيْ هُرَيْرَةَ رَضِيَ اللهُ عَنْهُ عَنِ النَّبِيِّ صَلَّى اللهُ
عَلَيْهِ وَسَلَّمَ قَالَ : مَنْ نَفَّسَ عَنْ مُؤْمِنٍ كُرْبَةً مِنْ كُرَبِ
الدُّنْيَا نَفَّسَ اللهُ عَنْهُ كُرْبَةً مِنْ كُرَبِ يَوْمِ الْقِيَامَةِ . . وَمَنْ
يَسَّرَ عَلَى مُعْسِرٍ يَسَّرَ اللهُ عَلَيْهِ فِي الدُّنْيَا وَالْآخِرَةِ . وَمَنْ
سَتَرَ مُسْلِمًا سَتَرَهُ اللهُ فِي الدُّنْيَا وَالْآخِرَةِ . وَاللهُ فِيْ عَوْنِ
الْعَبْدِ مَاكَانَ الْعَبْدُ فِيْ عَوْنِ أَخِيْهِ ، وَمَنْ سَلَكَ طَرِيْقًا
يَلْتَمِسُ فِيْهِ عِلْمًا سَهَّلَ اللهُ لَهُ بِهِ طَرِيْقًا إِلَى الْجَنَّةِ ،
وَمَااجْتَمَعَ قَوْمٌ فِيْ بَيْتٍ مِنْ بُيُوْتِ اللهِ يَتْلُوْنَ كِتَابَ اللهِ
وَيَتَدَارَسُوْنَهُ بَيْنَهُمْ إِلَّا نَزَلَتْ عَلَيْهِمُ السَّكِيْنَةُ وَغَشِيَتْهُمُ
الرَّحْمَةُ وَحَفَّتْهُمُ الْمَلَائِكَةُ وَذَكَرَهُمُ اللهُ فِيْمَنْ عِنْدَهُ . وَمَنْ
أَبْطَأَبِهِ عَمَلُهُ لَمْ يُسْرِعْ بِهِ نَسَبُهُ – رَوَاهُ مُسْلِمٌ بِهٰذَا اللَّفْظِ .

Translation:

It was related on the authority of Abū Hurayrah (*radiyallāhu 'anhu*) that the Prophet (*sallallāhu 'alayhi wasallam*) said, "Whosoever dispels from a believer some grief pertaining to this world, Allah will dispel from him some grief pertaining to the Day of Rising. Whoever makes things easy for someone who is in difficulties, Allah will make things easy for him both in this life and the next. Whosoever conceals

(the fault of) a Muslim, Allah will conceal (his faults) in this world and the next. Allah is ready to help a servant so long as the servant is ready to help his brother. Whosoever walks a path to seek knowledge therein, Allah will make easy for him thereby a path to the Garden. No community ever assembles in one of Allah's houses to recite Allah's Book and carefully study it among themselves but tranquillity descends to them, and mercy covers them, and the angels surround them, and Allah makes mention of them among those who are with Him. He whose work detains him will not be hastened by his (noble) ancestry."[1]
[Muslim relates it in these words.]

Notes:

1. The last lines stress the importance of good actions as the only means of salvation. No pride of ancestry, or nobility of lineage can make up for the slackness and deficiencies in good action. The verdict of the Qur'an is absolute in this respect: *Surely the noblest of you in the sight of Allah is (he who is) the most righteous of you* (Qur'an, 49:13).

عَنِ ابْنِ عَبَّاسٍ رَضِيَ اللهُ عَنْهُمَا عَنْ رَسُوْلِ اللهِ صَلَّى اللهُ عَلَيْهِ وَسَلَّمَ فِيْمَا يَرْوِيْهِ عَنْ رَبِّهِ تَبَارَكَ وَتَعَالَى قَالَ: إِنَّ اللهَ كَتَبَ الْحَسَنَاتِ وَالسَّيِّئَاتِ، ثُمَّ بَيَّنَ ذَلِكَ. فَمَنْ هَمَّ بِحَسَنَةٍ فَلَمْ يَعْمَلْهَا كَتَبَهَا اللهُ عِنْدَهُ حَسَنَةً كَامِلَةً، وَإِنْ هَمَّ بِهَا فَعَمِلَهَا كَتَبَهَا اللهُ عِنْدَهُ عَشْرَ حَسَنَاتٍ إِلَى سَبْعِمِائَةِ ضِعْفٍ إِلَى أَضْعَافٍ كَثِيْرَةٍ. وَإِنْ هَمَّ بِسَيِّئَةٍ فَلَمْ يَعْمَلْهَا كَتَبَهَا اللهُ عِنْدَهُ حَسَنَةً كَامِلَةً، وَإِنْ هَمَّ بِهَا فَعَمِلَهَا كَتَبَهَا اللهُ سَيِّئَةً وَاحِدَةً. رَوَاهُ الْبُخَارِيُّ وَمُسْلِمٌ فِيْ صَحِيْحَيْهِمَا بِهَذِهِ الْحُرُوْفِ ٭فَانْظُرْ يَاأَخِيْ وَفَّقَنَا اللهُ وَإِيَّاكَ إِلَى عَظِيمِ لُطْفِ اللهِ تَعَالَى وَتَأَمَّلْ هَذِهِ الْأَلْفَاظَ. وَقَوْلُهُ (عِنْدَهُ) إِشَارَةٌ إِلَى الْإِعْتِنَاءِ بِهَا. وَقَوْلُهُ (كَامِلَةً) لِلتَّأْكِيْدِ وَشِدَّةِ الْإِعْتِنَاءِ بِهَا. وَقَالَ فِي السَّيِّئَةِ الَّتِي هَمَّ بِهَا ثُمَّ تَرَكَهَا كَتَبَهَا اللهُ عِنْدَهُ حَسَنَةً كَامِلَةً فَأَكَّدَهَا بِكَامِلَةٍ، وَإِنْ عَمِلَهَا كَتَبَهَا سَيِّئَةً وَاحِدَةً فَأَكَّدَ تَقْلِيلَهَا بِوَاحِدَةٍ وَلَمْ يُؤَكِّدْهَا بِكَامِلَةٍ. فَلِلّهِ الْحَمْدُ وَالْمِنَّةُ سُبْحَانَهُ لَانُحْصِيْ ثَنَاءً عَلَيْهِ. وَبِاللهِ التَّوْفِيْقُ.

68

Ibn 'Abbās (*radiyallahu anhumā*) reported that the Messenger of Allah (*sallallāhu 'alayhi wasallam*) related from his Lord - blessed and exalted be He!: "Truly Allah has written down the good deeds and the evil deeds." Then he clarified that. "Whosoever intends to do a good deed but does not do it, Allah writes it down with Him as a complete good deed, but if he intends it and does it, Allah writes it down with Him as ten good deeds, up to seven hundred fold, or more than that manifold. But if he intends an evil deed and does not do it, Allah writes it down with Him as a complete good deed, and if he intends it and does it, Allah writes it down as one single evil deed."
[Al-Bukhārī and Muslim.]

Each in his *Sahīh*, have thus related it in these words:

"So look! My brother, may Allah help us, and take note of how great is the kindness of Allah - may He be exalted! Reflect on this, how that His saying 'with Him' points to His great care with regard to it, and His saying 'complete' is for emphasis, not to (point to) the intensity of His care with regard to it. With regard to the evil deed which one intended, but then abandoned, He says: 'Allah writes it down with Him as a complete good deed,' emphasising this by (the word) 'complete' (*kāmilah*); whereas if he performs it He writes it down as 'one evil deed', where by the word 'one' He emphasises its being made little of, since He does not emphasise it here by the word 'complete'. So to Allah be praise and grace. Glory be to Him! Our praises to Him we cannot count. With Allah is success (*wabillāhi tawfīq*)."[1]

Notes:

1. *Tawfīq* signifies conformation, adaptation, accommodation;

balancing, adjustment, settlement; reconciliation, mediation, arbitration, peacemaking, re-establishment of normal relations; success (granted by God), happy outcome, good fortune, good luck, prosperity, successfulness, succeeding.

عَنْ أَبِيْ هُرَيْرَةَ رَضِيَ اللهُ عَنْهُ قَالَ، قَالَ رَسُوْلُ اللهِ
صَلَّى اللهُ عَلَيْهِ وَسَلَّمَ: إِنَّ اللهَ تَعَالَى قَالَ: مَنْ عَادَى لِيْ
وَلِيًّا فَقَدْ آذَنْتُهُ بِالْحَرْبِ، وَمَاتَقَرَّبَ إِلَيَّ عَبْدِيْ بِشَيْءٍ أَحَبَّ
إِلَيَّ مِمَّا افْتَرَضْتُهُ عَلَيْهِ، وَلَا يَزَالُ عَبْدِيْ يَتَقَرَّبُ إِلَيَّ
بِالنَّوَافِلِ حَتَّى أُحِبَّهُ، فَإِذَا أَحْبَبْتُهُ كُنْتُ سَمْعَهُ الَّذِيْ
يَسْمَعُ بِهِ، وَبَصَرَهُ الَّذِيْ يُبْصِرُ بِهِ، وَيَدَهُ الَّتِيْ يَبْطِشُ بِهَا،
وَرِجْلَهُ الَّتِيْ يَمْشِيْ بِهَا، وَلَئِنْ سَأَلَنِيْ لَأُعْطِيَنَّهُ، وَلَئِنِ
اسْتَعَاذَنِيْ لَأُعِيْذَنَّهُ - رَوَاهُ الْبُخَارِيُّ.

Translation:

Abū Hurayrah (*radiyallāhu 'anhu*) reported that the
Messenger of Allah (*sallallāhu 'alayhi wasallam*) said,
"Truly Allah - may He be exalted - has said: 'Whosoever
acts with enmity towards a friend of Mine, against him will
I indeed declare war. Nothing endears My servant to Me
than doing of what I have made obligatory upon him to do.
And My servant ceases not seeking My nearness by offering
supererogatory (*nawāfil*) prayers till I love him. When I love
him, I shall be his hearing with which he shall hear, his
sight with which he shall see, his hands with which he shall
hold, and his feet with which he shall walk; and if he asks
Me, I shall surely give him, and if he takes refuge in Me, I

shall certainly give him refuge'."[1]
[Al-Bukhārī relates it.]

Note:

1.   Of course the love of Allah is all-embracing and includes the love of His Prophet. The Omnipotent Allah Who is "nearer to man than his jugular vein", responds when man calls Him earnestly. When a stage of complete identification is reached, the man is exalted and becomes one with His Lord, then Allah becomes his sight, his hearing, his limbs. This was demonstrated when the companions of the Prophet took an oath to stand fast with him: *Those who swear allegiance to thee do but swear allegiance to Allah. The hand of Allah is above their hands* (Qur'an, 48:10).
   Allah showed His mercy and gave His help to the Prophet and his companions in the battles against the godless forces of paganism. The Muslims were in very small numbers, but in their struggle against the superior force of pagans, and later against the might of the Byzantine and Persian Empires they succeeded by the grace of God.

Hadīth 39

اَلْحَدِيْثُ التَّاسِعُ وَالثَّلَاثُوْنَ

عَنِ ابْنِ عَبَّاسٍ رَضِيَ اللهُ عَنْهُمَا أَنَّ رَسُوْلَ اللهِ صَلَّى
اللهُ عَلَيْهِ وَسَلَّمَ قَالَ : إِنَّ اللهَ تَجَاوَزَ لِيْ عَنْ أُمَّتِيْ الْخَطَأَ
وَالنِّسْيَانَ وَمَااسْتُكْرِهُوْا عَلَيْهِ . حَدِيْثٌ حَسَنٌ . رَوَاهُ ابْنُ
مَاجَهْ وَالْبَيْهَقِيُّ وَغَيْرُهُمَا .

Translation:

Ibn 'Abbās (*radiyallahu anhumā*) reported that the Messenger of Allah (*sallallāhu 'alayhi wasallam*) said, "Truly Allah has for my sake overlooked the mistakes and forgetfulness of my community, and what were forced upon them."[1]

[An excellent Ḥadīth which Ibn Mājah and al-Bayhaqī and others have related.]

Notes:

1. Surely, the Holy Prophet by Divine grace shall intercede on behalf of the sinners, and this special privilege of the Prophet *sallallāhu 'alayhi wasallam* is referred to in the following verses of the Qur'an: *And those whom they call upon besides Him have no power of intercession - only he who bears witness to the Truth and they know (him)* (43:86).

In another place it is said: *O Prophet, surely We have sent thee as a witness, and a bearer of good news and a warner. And as inviter to Allah by His permission, and as a light giving sun. And give the believers the good news that they will have great grace from Allah* (33:45-47). And again: *Certainly a Messenger has come to you from yourselves; grievous to him is your falling into distress, most solicitous for you, to the believers (he is)*

73

compassionate, merciful (9:128).

There are two courses open for a Muslim, either to lay down his life, rather than submit to what is against his belief and conscience - and this is the best - or to submit to compulsion, and then seek His forgiveness for Allah knows what is manifest and hidden. The Qur'an teaches the believers to pray: *Our Lord, punish us not if we forget or make a mistake. Our Lord, do not lay on us a burden as Thou didst lay on those before us. Our Lord, impose not on us (afflictions) which we have not the strength to bear. And pardon us! And grant us protection! And have mercy on us! Thou art our Patron, so grant us victory over the disbelieving people* (2:286).

عَنِ ابْنِ عُمَرَ رَضِيَ اللهُ عَنْهُمَا قَالَ : أَخَذَ رَسُوْلُ اللهِ
صَلَّى اللهُ عَلَيْهِ وَسَلَّمَ بِمَنْكِبِيْ . فَقَالَ : كُنْ فِي الدُّنْيَا كَأَنَّكَ
غَرِيْبٌ أَوْ عَابِرُ سَبِيْلٍ . وَكَانَ ابْنُ عُمَرَ رَضِيَ اللهُ عَنْهُمَا
يَقُوْلُ : إِذَا أَمْسَيْتَ فَلَاتَنْتَظِرِ الصَّبَاحَ، وَإِذَا أَصْبَحْتَ
فَلَاتَنْتَظِرِ الْمَسَاءَ، وَخُذْ مِنْ صِحَّتِكَ لِمَرَضِكَ وَمِنْ حَيَاتِكَ
لِمَوْتِكَ - رَوَاهُ الْبُخَارِيُّ .

Translation:

From Ibn 'Umar   (*radiyallahu anhumā*) who said: The
Messenger of Allah (*sallallāhu 'alayhi wasallam*) took me by
the shoulder and said: "Be in this world as though you were
a stranger or a traveller."

Ibn 'Umar used to say: When evening comes on you,
do not expect morning, and when morning comes on you, do
not expect evening. Take from your health (a preparation)
for your sickness, and from your life for your death.
[Al-Bukhārī relates this.]

عَنْ أَبِيْ مُحَمَّدٍ عَبْدِ اللهِ بْنِ عَمْرِو بْنِ الْعَاصِ رَضِيَ
اللهُ عَنْهُمَا قَالَ . قَالَ رَسُوْلُ اللهِ صَلَّى اللهُ عَلَيْهِ وَسَلَّمَ :
لَا يُؤْمِنُ أَحَدُكُمْ حَتَّى يَكُوْنَ هَوَاهُ تَبَعًا لِمَا جِئْتُ بِهِ .
حَدِيْثٌ صَحِيْحٌ . رَوَيْنَاهُ فِيْ كِتَابِ الْحُجَّةِ بِإِسْنَادٍ
صَحِيْحٍ .

Translation:

Abū Muhammad 'Abdullāh bin 'Amr bin al-'Ās (*radiyallahu anhumā*) reported that the Messenger of Allah (*sallallāhu 'alayhi wasallam*) said: "No one of you (truly) believes until his desire follows that with which I have come."[1]

[It is an excellent Ḥadīth, and a genuine one, which we have related from the *Kitāb al-Hujjah*, with a genuine *isnād*. (*Kitāb al-Hujjah* is the work of Abū al-Qāsim Ismaʿīl bin Muhammad bin al-Fadl al-Asfahāni, who was a *Faqīh* and pious and much devoted to Allah. This work discusses *iʿtiqad*, or doctrine of *Ahl al-Sunnah*).]

Note:

1.   The faith is clear and its practice was made into an example by the Prophet *sallallāhu 'alayhi wasallam*. It is the duty of the faithful to follow the *Sunnah* of the Prophet in true spirit, and not to distort the teachings of the Qur'an or the *Sunnah* of the Prophet to suit their own desires, appetites and ambitions. *And it behoves not a believing man or a believing woman, when Allah and His Messenger have decided an affair, to exercise a choice in the matter. And whoever disobeys Allah and His Messenger, he surely strays off to manifest error (33:36).*

76

عَنْ أَنَسٍ رَضِيَ اللهُ عَنْهُ قَالَ: سَمِعْتُ رَسُوْلَ اللهِ
صَلَّى اللهُ عَلَيْهِ وَسَلَّمَ يَقُوْلُ؛ قَالَ اللهُ تَعَالَى: يَاابْنَ آدَمَ!
إِنَّكَ مَادَعَوْتَنِيْ وَرَجَوْتَنِيْ غَفَرْتُ لَكَ عَلَى مَاكَانَ مِنْكَ وَلَا
أُبَالِيْ. يَاابْنَ آدَمَ! لَوْ بَلَغَتْ ذُنُوْبُكَ عِنَانَ السَّمَاءِ ثُمَّ
اسْتَغْفَرْتَنِيْ غَفَرْتُ لَكَ. يَاابْنَ آدَمَ! إِنَّكَ لَوْ أَتَيْتَنِيْ بِقُرَابِ
الْأَرْضِ خَطَايَا ثُمَّ لَقِيْتَنِيْ لَاتُشْرِكُ بِيْ شَيْئًا لَأَتَيْتُكَ بِقُرَابِهَا
مَغْفِرَةً - رَوَاهُ التِّرْمِذِيُّ وَقَالَ: حَدِيْثٌ حَسَنٌ صَحِيْحٌ.

Translation:

From Anas (*radiyallāhu 'anhu*) who said: I heard the
Messenger of Allah (*sallallāhu 'alayhi wasallam*) say, "Allah
- may He be exalted - has said: 'O son of Adam, so long as
you call upon Me, and hope in Me, I will forgive you for all
that comes from you, and I do not care. O son of Adam, if
your sins were to reach even the farthest heights (clouds) in
the sky, and you asked for My forgiveness, I shall forgive
you. O son of Adam, were you to come to Me with an
earthful of sins and met Me without having associated
anything with Me, I shall grant you an earthful of pardon'".[1]
[Al-Tirmidhī relates it, saying: It is an excellent, genuine Hadīth.]

Note:

1. This Hadīth reiterates and warns the believers to avoid

any semblance of *shirk,* which would nullify all good actions, and forfeit all hopes of Allah's mercy. In case a person is not guilty of *shirk*, his sins however enormous and grave maybe, will be forgiven by Allah in His boundless mercy.

> *Say: O my servants who have transgressed against their souls! Despair not of the Mercy of Allah: for Allah forgives all sins for He is Oft-Forgiving, Most Merciful* (Qur'an, 39:53).